Think Good – Feel Good

A Cognitive Behaviour Therapy Workbook for Children and Young People

Paul Stallard
Consultant Clinical Psychologist, Royal United Hospital, Bath, UK

JOHN WILEY & SONS, LTD

Copyright © 2002   John Wiley & Sons Ltd, The Atrium, Southern Gate, Chichester, West Sussex PO19 8SQ, England

Telephone   (+44) 1243 779777

Email (for orders and customer service enquiries): cs-books@wiley.co.uk
Visit our Home Page on www.wileyeurope.com or www.wiley.co.uk

24 2017

This publication is designed to provide accurate and authoritative information in regard to the subject matter covered. It is sold on the understanding that the Publisher is not engaged in rendering professional services. If professional advice or other expert assistance is required, the services of a competent professional should be sought.

Other Wiley Editorial Offices

John Wiley & Sons Inc., 111 River Street, Hoboken, NJ 07030, USA

Jossey-Bass, 989 Market Street, San Francisco, CA 94103-1741, USA

Wiley-VCH Verlag GmbH, Boschstr. 12, D-69469 Weinheim, Germany

John Wiley & Sons Australia Ltd, 33 Park Road, Milton, Queensland 4064, Australia

John Wiley & Sons (Asia) Pte Ltd, 2 Clementi Loop #02-01, Jin Xing Distripark, Singapore 129809

John Wiley & Sons Canada Ltd, 22 Worcester Road, Etobicoke, Ontario, Canada M9W 1L1

British Library Cataloguing in Publication Data

A catalogue record for this book is available from the British Library

ISBN 978-0-470-84290-4 (PB)

Typeset in 12/15 Scala Sans by Mathematical Composition Setters Ltd, Salisbury, Wiltshire
Printed and bound in Great Britain by TJ International, Padstow, Cornwall

Contents

About the author

Dr Paul Stallard graduated as a clinical psychologist from Birmingham University in 1980. He worked with children and young people in the West Midlands before moving to the Department of Child and Family Psychiatry, Bath, in 1988. He is a visiting research fellow at Bath University, and has received a number of research grants exploring the effects of trauma and chronic illness on children. He has published over 50 peer-reviewed papers and is currently leading a research trial exploring the use of cognitive behaviour therapy in the treatment of post-traumatic stress disorders.

On-Line Resources

All the text and workbook resources in this book are **available free, in colour, to purchasers** of the print version. Visit the website **http://www.wileyeurope.com/go/thinkgoodfeelgood** to find out how to access and download these flexible aids to working with your clients. The on-line facility provides an opportunity to download and print relevant sections of the workbook that can then be used in clinical sessions with children. The on-line materials are in colour, which may prove more attractive and interesting to younger children. The materials can be used flexibly, and can be accessed and used as often as required.

In addition to the printed medium, *Think Good – Feel Good* can be used as an interactive computer programme. The on-line version of *Think Good – Feel Good* can be downloaded and the exercises completed and saved on a computer. This may be particularly appealing to adolescents and computer-minded children who may be more motivated and interested in using this format. The materials can be used to structure or supplement clinical sessions or can be completed by the young person at home. Relevant sections of the workbook can be given to children on floppy disc to take home, which can then be reviewed during clinical sessions with the therapist.

Finally, the therapist is also able to edit some of the worksheets so that the exercises can be tailored to the particular child. For example, the therapist could edit and amend the "IF/THEN quiz" or "common beliefs" and type in their own questions for the child to answer. The completed forms can then be printed, saved and used as many times as required.

CHAPTER ONE

Cognitive behaviour therapy: theoretical origins, rationale and techniques

Cognitive behaviour therapy (CBT) is a term used to describe psychotherapeutic interventions that aim to reduce psychological distress and maladaptive behaviour by altering cognitive processes (Kaplan *et al.*, 1995). CBT is based on the underlying assumption that affect and behaviour are largely a product of cognitions and, as such, that cognitive and behavioural interventions can bring about changes in thinking, feeling and behaviour (Kendall, 1991). CBT therefore embraces the core elements of both cognitive and behavioural theories, and has been defined by Kendall and Hollon (1979) as seeking to:

> preserve the efficacy of behavioural techniques but within a less doctrinaire context that takes account of the child's cognitive interpretations and attributions about events.

There is growing interest in the use of CBT with children and young people. This interest has been encouraged by a number of reviews which have concluded that CBT is a promising and effective intervention for the treatment of child psychological problems (Kazdin and Weisz, 1998; Roth and Fonagy, 1996; Wallace *et al.*, 1995). CBT has been found to be effective in treating generalized anxiety disorders (Kendall, 1994; Kendall *et al.*, 1997; Silverman *et al.*, 1999a), depressive disorders (Harrington *et al.*, 1998; Lewinsohn and Clarke, 1999), interpersonal problems and social phobia (Spence and Donovan, 1998; Spence *et al.*, 2000), phobias (Silverman *et al.*, 1999b), school refusal (King *et al.*, 1998) and sexual abuse (Cohen and Mannarino, 1996, 1998), and in the management of pain (Sanders *et al.*, 1994). In addition, CBT has been advocated as producing positive effects with a range of other problems, including adolescent conduct (Herbert, 1998), eating (Schmidt, 1998), post-traumatic stress (March *et al.*, 1998; Smith *et al.*, 1999) and obsessive-compulsive disorders (March, 1995; March *et al.*, 1994).

Cognitive behaviour therapy focuses on the relationship between the following:

■ cognitions (what we think);

■ affect (how we feel);

■ behaviour (what we do).

Cognitive behaviour therapy has demonstrated positive effects in the treatment of a number of common child psychological problems.

▶ The empirical foundations of cognitive behaviour therapy

The theoretical basis for cognitive behaviour therapy has evolved through a number of significant research influences. A review of this research is beyond the remit of this book, although it is important to note some of the key concepts and approaches that have underpinned and shaped CBT.

One of the earliest influences was that of Pavlov and classical conditioning. Pavlov highlighted how, with repeated pairings, naturally occurring responses (e.g. salivation) could become associated (i.e. conditioned) with specific stimuli (e.g. the sound of a bell). This research demonstrated that emotional responses (e.g. fear) could become conditioned by specific events and situations.

> ■ Emotional responses can become conditioned to specific events.

Classical conditioning was extended to human behaviour and clinical problems by Wolpe (1958), who developed the procedure of systematic desensitization. By pairing fear-inducing stimuli with a second stimulus that produces an antagonistic response (i.e. relaxation), the fear response can be reciprocally inhibited. The procedure is now widely used in clinical practice and involves graded exposure, both *in vivo* and in imagination, to a hierarchy of feared situations whilst remaining relaxed.

> ■ Emotional responses can be reciprocally inhibited.

The second major behavioural influence was the work of Skinner (1974), who highlighted the significant role of environmental influences in behaviour. This became known as operant conditioning, and focused on the relationship between antecedents (setting conditions), consequences (reinforcement) and behaviour. In essence, if a certain behaviour increases in frequency because it is followed by positive consequences, or is not followed by negative consequences, then that behaviour has been reinforced.

> ■ Behaviour is affected by antecedents and consequences.
> ■ Consequences that increase the likelihood of a behaviour are reinforcers.
> ■ Altering antecedents and consequences can result in changes in behaviour.

An important extension of behavioural therapy to account for the mediating role of cognitive processes was proposed by Albert Bandura (1977), with the development of social learning theory. The importance of the environment was recognized, while at the same time the mediating effect of the cognitions that intervene between stimuli and response was highlighted. The theory emphasized that learning could occur by watching someone else, and it proposed a model of self-control based on self-observation, self-evaluation and self-reinforcement.

A more significant focus on cognitions emerged from the work of Meichenbaum (1975) and the development of self-instructional training. This approach highlighted the concept that much behaviour is under the control of thoughts or internal speech. Changing self-instructions can lead to the development of more appropriate self-control techniques. The model adopts a developmental perspective and reflects the process by which children learn to control their behaviour. A four-stage process involving observing someone else undertaking a task, being talked through the same task by another person, talking oneself through the task out loud, and finally whispering instructions/silent talk, was described.

> ■ Behaviour is influenced by cognitive events and processes.
> ■ Changing cognitive processes can lead to changes in behaviour.

The link between emotions and cognitions was outlined by Albert Ellis (1962) in rational emotive therapy. This model proposed that emotion and behaviour arise from the way in which events are construed, rather than by the event *per se*. Thus activating events (A) are assessed against beliefs (B) which result in emotional consequences (C). Beliefs can be either rational or irrational, with negative emotional states tending to arise from and be maintained by irrational beliefs.

The role of maladaptive and distorted cognitions in the development and maintenance of depression was developed through the work of Aaron Beck, culminating in the publication of *Cognitive Therapy for Depression* (Beck, 1976; Beck *et al.*, 1979). The model proposes that maladaptive thoughts about the self, the world and the future (cognitive triad) result in cognitive distortions which create negative affect. Particular attention is payed to core assumptions or schemas – that is, the fairly fixed beliefs developed in childhood against which events are assessed. Once activated, these fixed beliefs produce a range of automatic thoughts. These automatic thoughts and beliefs may be subject to a range of distortions or logical errors, with more negative cognitions being associated with depressed mood.

- ■ Emotional affect is influenced by cognitions.
- ■ Irrational beliefs/schemas or negative cognitions are associated with negative affect.
- ■ Altering cognitive processes can lead to changes in affect.

The relationship between cognitive processes and other emotional states and psychological problems has now been documented (Beck *et al.*, 1985; Hawton *et al.*, 1989). More recent interest has led to further exploration of the relationship between beliefs/schemas in the development and maintenance of psychological problems. This is encapsulated in the schema-focused work of Young (1990), who proposed that maladaptive cognitive schemas that are formed during childhood lead to self-defeating patterns of behaviour which are repeated throughout life. The maladaptive schemas are associated with certain parenting styles, and they develop if the basic emotional needs of the child are not met. Evidence to support the presence of 15 primary schemas has been reported (Schmidt *et al.*, 1995).

- ■ Maladaptive cognitive schemas develop during childhood, and may be associated with parenting styles.

Empirical testing of this prediction is still required. However, if substantiated, it would set an exciting challenge for child workers in identifying whether more adaptive cognitive processes can be promoted and future mental health problems minimized.

▶ The cognitive model

Cognitive behaviour therapy is concerned with understanding how events and experiences are interpreted, and with identifying and changing the distortions or deficits that occur in cognitive processing.

Based largely on the work of Aaron Beck, the way in which dysfunctional cognitive processes are acquired, activated and affect behaviour and emotions is summarized diagrammatically in the model shown in Figure 1.1.

Early experiences and parenting are postulated to lead to the development of fairly fixed and rigid ways of thinking (i.e. core beliefs/schemas). New information and experiences are assessed against these core beliefs/schemas (e.g. 'I must be successful'), and information that reinforces and maintains them is selected and filtered. Core beliefs/schemas are triggered or activated by important events (e.g. taking exams), and these lead to a number of assumptions

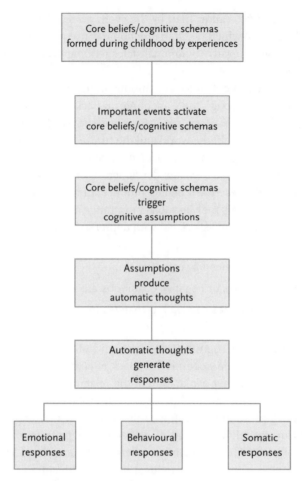

Figure 1.1   The cognitive model.

(e.g. 'I can only get a good mark if I study all day'). These in turn give rise to a stream of automatic thoughts which are related to the person (e.g. 'I must be stupid'), their performance (e.g. 'I'm not working hard enough') and the future ('I'll never pass these exams and get to university'), often referred to as the cognitive triad. In turn, these automatic thoughts can result in emotional changes (e.g. anxiety, sadness), behavioural changes (e.g. staying in, constantly working) and somatic changes (e.g. loss of appetite, difficulty in sleeping).

▶ Cognitive deficits and distortions

Cognitive behaviour therapy assumes that psychopathology is a result of abnormalities in cognitive processing. In particular, difficulties are assumed to be associated with cognitive distortions or deficits.

Cognitive distortions have been reported in children with a range of difficulties. Children with anxiety disorders have been found to misperceive ambiguous events as threatening (Kendall *et al.*, 1992). They tend to be overly self-focused and hypercritical, and to report increased levels of self-talk and negative expectations (Kendall and Panichelli-Mindel, 1995). Similarly, aggressive children perceive more aggressive intent in ambiguous situations, and selectively attend to fewer cues when making decisions about the intent of another person's behaviour (Dodge, 1985). Depressed children have been found to make more negative attributions than non-depressed children, and they are more likely to attribute negative events to internal stable causes and positive events to external unstable causes (Bodiford *et al.*, 1988; Curry and Craighead, 1990). They have distorted perceptions of their own performance, and they selectively attend to the negative features of events (Kendall *et al.*, 1990; Leitenberg *et al.*, 1986; Rehm and Carter, 1990).

Interventions that address cognitive distortions are concerned with increasing the child's awareness of dysfunctional and irrational cognitions, beliefs and schemas, and with facilitating their understanding of the effects of these upon behaviour and emotions. Programmes typically involve some form of self-monitoring, identification of maladaptive cognitions, thought testing and cognitive restructuring.

Deficits in cognitive processes, such as an inability to engage in planning or problem solving, have been found in children and young people with problems of self-control such as attention deficit hyperactivity disorder (ADHD), and also in children with interpersonal difficulties (Kendall, 1993; Spence and Donovan, 1998). For example, aggressive children have been found to possess limited problem-solving skills and generate fewer verbal solutions to difficulties (Lochman *et al.*, 1991; Perry *et al.*, 1986). Children with social phobia have been found to present with social skill deficits, and antisocial children demonstrate poor social perception skills (Chandler, 1973; Spence *et al.*, 1999).

Cognitive behaviour therapy interventions that address cognitive deficits are primarily concerned with the teaching of new cognitive and behavioural skills. Programmes often involve social problem solving, learning new cognitive strategies (e.g. self-instructional training and positive/coping self-talk), practice and self-reinforcement.

Understanding how children and young people cognitively interpret events and experiences is a fundamental requirement of CBT, and should inform the nature of the cognitive intervention that is provided. However, comparatively little is known about the cognitive deficits or distortions that underpin many childhood problems. Advances in work with adults suffering from post-traumatic stress and obsessional-compulsive disorders highlight the importance of understanding the way in which the trauma or compulsion is appraised (Ehlers and Clark, 2000; Salkovskis, 1999). Persistent post-traumatic stress disorder (PTSD) may be associated with distorted cognitive processes that result in the trauma being appraised as a serious current threat (Ehlers and Clark, 2000). Similarly, the cognitions that underpin many obsessive-compulsive disorders relate to distorted cognitions and appraisals regarding an inflated responsibility for harm (Salkovskis, 1999). Whether these distortions also apply to children has not yet been determined, although it is clear that further work is required to improve our understanding of the cognitive processes that underlie the psychological problems and disorders of children.

> ▪ Children with psychological problems present with cognitive deficits and distortions.
> ▪ There is a need to understand more about the cognitive processes associated with psychological problems in children.

▶ Core characteristics of cognitive behaviour therapy

The term *cognitive behaviour therapy* is used to describe a range of different interventions, although they often share a number of core features (Fennel, 1989).

CBT is theoretically determined

CBT is based on empirically testable models which provide both the rationale for the intervention (i.e. that affect and behaviour are largely determined by cognitions) and the focus and nature of the intervention (i.e. challenging distortions or rectifying deficiencies). CBT is a cohesive, rational intervention – not simply a collection of disparate techniques.

CBT is based on a collaborative model

A key feature of CBT is the collaborative process by which it occurs. The young person has an active role with regard to identifying their goals, setting targets, experimenting, practising and monitoring their performance. The approach is designed to facilitate greater and more effective self-control, with the therapist providing a supportive framework within which this can occur. The role of the therapist is to develop a partnership in which the young person is empowered to achieve a better understanding of their problems and to discover alternative ways of thinking and behaving.

CBT is time limited

It is brief and time limited, often consisting of no more than 16 sessions, and in many cases far fewer than this. The brief nature of the intervention promotes independence and encourages self-help. This model is readily applicable to work with children and adolescents, for whom the typical period of intervention is considerably shorter than that for adults.

CBT is objective and structured

It is a structured and objective approach that guides the young person through a process of assessment, problem formulation, intervention, monitoring and evaluation. The goals and targets of the intervention are explicitly defined and regularly reviewed. There is an emphasis on quantification and the use of ratings (e.g. the frequency of inappropriate behaviour, strength of belief in dysfunctional thoughts or degree of distress experienced). Regular monitoring and review provide a means of assessing progress by comparing current performance against baseline assessments.

CBT has a here-and-now focus

CBT interventions focus on the present, dealing with current problems and difficulties. They do not seek to 'uncover unconscious early trauma or biological, neurological and genetic contributions to psychological dysfunction, but instead strive to build a new, more adaptive way to process the world' (Kendall and Panichelli-Mindel, 1995). This approach has high face validity for children and young people, who may be more interested in and motivated to address real-time, here-and-now issues, rather than understanding their origins.

CBT is based on a process of guided self-discovery and experimentation

It is an active process that encourages self-questioning and challenging of assumptions and beliefs. The client is not simply a passive recipient of therapist advice or observations, but is encouraged to challenge and learn through a process of experimentation. The validity of thoughts, assumptions and beliefs is tested, alternative explanations are discovered, and new ways of appraising events and behaving are tried and assessed.

CBT is a skills-based approach

CBT provides a practical, skills-based approach to learning alternative patterns of thinking and behaviour. Young people are encouraged to practise skills and ideas that are discussed during therapy sessions in their everyday life, with home practice tasks being a core element of many programmes.

- ■ CBT is theoretically determined.
- ■ It is based on a model of active collaboration.
- ■ It is brief and time limited.
- ■ It is objective and structured.
- ■ It focuses on current problems.
- ■ It encourages self-discovery and experimentation.
- ■ It advocates a skills-based learning approach.

▶ The goal of cognitive behaviour therapy

The overall purpose of cognitive behaviour therapy is to increase self-awareness, facilitate better self-understanding, and improve self-control by developing more appropriate cognitive and behavioural skills. CBT helps to identify dysfunctional thoughts and beliefs that are predominantly negative, biased and self-critical. Processes of self-monitoring, education, experimentation and testing result in these thoughts and beliefs being replaced by more positive, balanced and functional cognitions that acknowledge strengths and success. Cognitive and behavioural deficits are identified, and new cognitive problem-solving skills and ways of behaving are learned, tested, evaluated and reinforced. A greater understanding of the nature of and reasons underlying unpleasant feelings is developed as they are replaced by more pleasant emotions. Finally, new cognitive and behavioural skills allow new and difficult situations to be confronted successfully in a more appropriate way.

The process helps to move the young person from a dysfunctional cycle to a more functional cycle as illustrated in Figure 1.2.

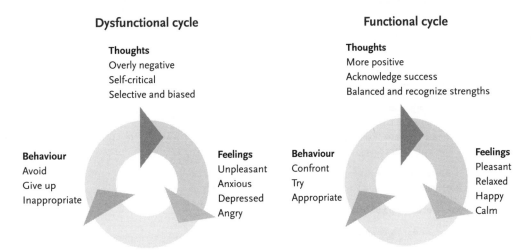

Figure 1.2 Functional and dysfunctional cycles.

▶ The core components of cognitive behavioural interventions

Given the variety of influences that have contributed to the development of cognitive behaviour therapy, it is not surprising that it has become an umbrella term used to describe a range of techniques and strategies that are utilized in different sequences and permutations. The specific components of the intervention should be determined by the problem formulation, which will inform the focus and nature of the programme. Interventions should be tailored to particular problems and the individual needs of the child, rather than being delivered in a standardized 'cookery book' approach. Although this flexibility is welcomed, it has also led to confusion with regard to which interventions are CBT and which are not.

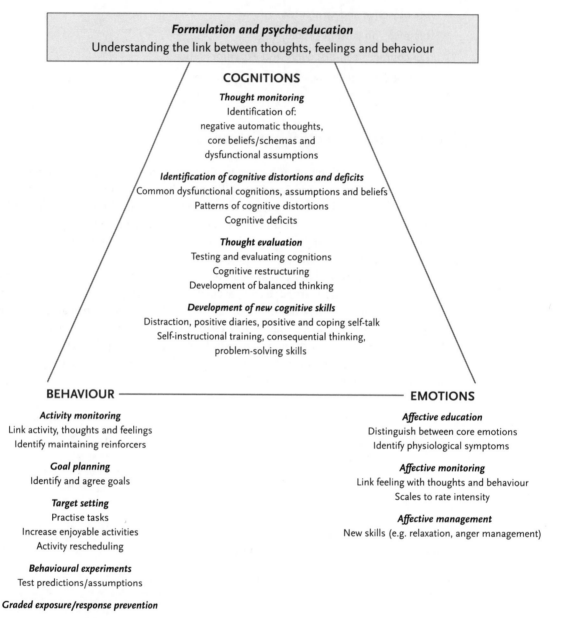

Figure 1.3 The clinician's toolbox.

The approaches that are advocated as falling under this general umbrella vary considerably in their emphasis on cognitive or behavioural interventions, and it can sometimes be difficult to identify the cognitive component. For example, interventions with children and young people with obsessive-compulsive disorder tend to be primarily behavioural in orientation, emphasizing psycho-education, anxiety management, graded exposure and response prevention (March, 1995). The cognitive component tends to be extremely limited and may rely extensively on one set of cognitive strategies (e.g. positive self-talk or self-instructional training).

Although the relative emphasis on cognitive and behavioural elements and the specific treatment components may vary, cognitive behaviour therapy programmes often include many of the following.

Formulation and psychoeducation

A basic component of all cognitive behavioural programmes involves education about the link between *thoughts, feelings* and *behaviour*. The process involves developing a clear and shared understanding of the relationship between how people think, how they feel and what they do.

Thought monitoring

A key task is the identification of common cognitions and patterns of thinking. Thought monitoring could focus on *core beliefs, negative automatic thoughts* or *dysfunctional assumptions*, and it involves recording 'hot' situations (i.e. those that produce a strong emotional change or overly negative or self-critical thoughts). The *cognitive triad* provides a useful way of structuring and organizing information and assessing young people's thoughts about themselves, their world and what they do.

Identification of cognitive distortions and deficits

The process of thought monitoring provides an opportunity to identify common *negative or dysfunctional cognitions and irrational beliefs or assumptions*. In turn, this results in increased awareness of the nature and type of *cognitive distortions* (e.g. magnification, focusing on the negative), *cognitive deficits* (e.g. misinterpretation of others cues as negative, limited range of problem-solving skills) and the effect of these on mood and behaviour.

Thought evaluation and development of alternative cognitive processes

The identification of dysfunctional cognitive processes leads to the systematic *testing and evaluation of these assumptions and beliefs* and the learning of alternative cognitive skills. The development of a process of *balanced thinking* or *cognitive restructuring* is encouraged. This may involve a process of looking for new information, thinking from another person's perspective or looking for contradictory evidence, which may result in dysfunctional cognitions being revised.

The evaluation provides an opportunity to develop alternative, *more balanced* and *functional* cognitions, which recognize difficulties but acknowledge strengths and success.

Learning new cognitive skills

Programmes often involve the teaching of new cognitive skills. The range of skills is vast and could include *distraction, positive self-talk, self-instructional training, consequential thinking* and *problem-solving skills*.

Affective education

Most programmes involve emotional education that is designed to *identify and distinguish core emotions* such as anger, anxiety or unhappiness. Programmes often focus on the *physiological changes* associated with these emotions (e.g. dry mouth, sweaty hands, increased heart rate) in order to facilitate a greater awareness of the child's own distinctive personal expression of emotion.

Affective monitoring

The monitoring of strong or dominant emotions can help to identify *times, places, activities* or *thoughts* that are associated with both pleasant and unpleasant feelings. *Scales* are used to rate the intensity of emotion during both real-life situations and treatment sessions, and provide an objective way of monitoring performance and assessing change.

Affective management

Programmes that address problems in which there are high levels of arousal, such as anxiety, phobias and post-traumatic stress, usually provide *relaxation training*. This may involve techniques such as *progressive muscle relaxation, controlled breathing* or *calming imagery*.

Greater awareness of the individual's unique emotional pattern can lead to the development of *preventative strategies*. For example, an awareness of the anger build-up may enable a young person to stop the emotional progression at an earlier stage and thereby prevent aggressive outbursts.

Target setting and activity rescheduling

Target setting is an inherent part of all cognitive behavioural programmes. The *overall goals* of therapy are mutually agreed and defined in ways that can be objectively assessed. The transfer of skills from therapy sessions to everyday life is encouraged by the systematic use of *assignment tasks*. The achievement of *specified targets* is reviewed and provides an overview of progress.

Targets may involve *increasing activities* that produce more pleasant emotions or *rescheduling* everyday life to prevent or minimize those activities which are associated with strong unpleasant emotions.

Behavioural experiments

Cognitive behavioural therapy is based on a process of guided discovery during which assumptions and thoughts are challenged and tested. This may involve setting up *behavioural experiments* to determine whether what happens is similar or different to what was predicted.

Exposure

A process of *graduated exposure* that is designed to help to facilitate mastery of difficult situations or images is included in most programmes. Problem situations are defined, the overall task is broken down into smaller steps and then each is ranked in a hierarchy of ascending difficulty. Starting with the least difficult, the client is exposed to each step of the hierarchy, either *in vivo* or in imagination. Once one step has been successfully completed they move to the next step, progressing through the hierarchy until the problem has been mastered.

Role play, modelling and rehearsal

The learning of new skills and behaviours can be achieved in a variety of ways. *Role play* provides an opportunity to practise dealing with difficult or challenging situations such as coping with teasing. It enables positive skills to be identified and alternative solutions or new skills highlighted. A process of *skills enhancement* can facilitate the process of acquiring new skills and behaviours. Observing others *modelling appropriate behaviour* or skills can then result in new behaviour being *rehearsed in imagination* before being *practised in real life*.

Reinforcement and reward

A cornerstone of all cognitive behavioural programmes is the *positive reinforcement* of appropriate behaviour. This could take the form of *self-reinforcement* – for example, cognitively (e.g. 'Well done, I coped well with that situation'), materially (e.g. purchasing a special CD) or specific activities (e.g. a special relaxing bath). Positive reinforcement from others, particularly carers, is important for younger children, and can be encouraged by the use of *star charts*, *contingency contracts* or *token credit systems*.

> ■ The balance between cognitive and behavioural interventions varies considerably within CBT programmes.
> ■ The core components of many CBT programmes include the following:
> monitoring of thoughts, feelings and/or behaviour;
> psycho-education and problem formulation;
> identification, challenging and testing of cognitions;
> developing new cognitive skills;
> learning alternative ways to manage anxiety or unpleasant emotions;
> learning new behaviours;
> target setting and home-based practice assignments;
> positive reinforcement.

▶ A cautionary note

Although the growing interest in the use of cognitive behaviour therapy with children and young people is welcomed, it is important to acknowledge that the evidence and theoretical base for this client group is more limited than that for adults.

Evidence for effectiveness

Comparatively few well-designed treatment trials with children have been reported to date. A number of early studies demonstrating the effectiveness of cognitive behaviour therapy have been conducted on volunteers who may not be as severely impaired as clinic attenders (Weisz *et al.*, 1995). Comparatively little evaluation has been undertaken with clinical populations who may also present with multiple comorbid conditions. Replication across sites by other clinical and research teams to demonstrate the wider applicability of defined CBT interventions has seldom occurred. Relatively few randomized controlled trials have been undertaken (Harrington *et al.*, 1998; Kazdin and Weisz, 1998), and evidence demonstrating the medium- and long-term effectiveness of CBT is lacking (Graham, 1998). In conclusion, the results of randomized controlled treatment trials typically suggest that CBT is more effective than no intervention (i.e. waiting-list control groups), although the superiority of CBT over other psychotherapeutic interventions has yet to be consistently demonstrated.

Developmentally appropriate theoretical models

The theoretical basis of CBT and models of intervention have largely developed through work with adults. Although these models and techniques have been applied to children and young people, further research is required in order to test whether they are appropriate for this age group. For example, at what age do children develop distorted cognitions? And do child trauma sufferers make the same appraisals as adults?

Cognitive behaviour therapy is also grounded on the premise that interventions are based on testable underlying theoretical models that link problematic behaviour and emotions with cognitive processes. The filtration of adult-derived models down to children has resulted in developmentally appropriate theoretical cognitive models for explaining emotional and behavioural problems in children and young people being comparatively under-developed.

Assessing changes in cognitive processes

The success of CBT in bringing about changes in behaviour and emotions depends on altering cognitive processes (Spence, 1994). Although there may be occasions when cognitive interventions can be successful without assuming psychopathology to be a direct result of deficient cognitive skills, the need to focus more on cognitive outcomes is important. To date, CBT studies have largely focused on assessing behavioural outcomes, with postulated changes in cognitive processes seldom being directly assessed. This led Durlak *et al.* (1991) to conclude that:

> it would be disconcerting to find that cognitive variables which are emphasised in CBT programmes are not in some way related to outcomes.

The challenge for researchers is to develop appropriate ways of assessing children's cognitions. This will increase understanding of the deficits and/or distortions that underlie child psychological problems, and will allow testing of the premise that CBT results in changes in cognitive processes.

Definition of CBT with children

A fourth issue is that of definition and the need to clarify what cognitive behaviour therapy with children entails. As highlighted by Graham (1998), CBT encapsulates a wide and diverse range of techniques, and it is sometimes difficult to identify the core and shared elements of these programmes. At times, the 'cognitive' component is minimal, or it is limited to one specific technique, such as coping self-talk, with the predominant emphasis of most programmes being behavioural. Grouping such diverse programmes under the general umbrella of cognitive behavioural therapy could appear to be questionable. This lack of specificity leads to confusion, and the question of whether CBT is an effective intervention will remain unanswered unless the core elements of such programmes are defined.

Further work is required to:

- demonstrate the long-term effectiveness of CBT with clinical groups;
- devise developmentally appropriate theoretical models;
- assess assumed changes in cognitive processes;
- define the core features of CBT with children.

In summary, although the available evidence suggests that CBT can make an important contribution to the treatment of a wide range of emotional and behavioural problems, further well-designed research with clinical populations is required. There is a need to devise developmentally appropriate cognitive models for understanding child and adolescent emotional and behavioural problems, and to define more precisely what cognitive behaviour therapy with children entails. This will also help to determine what 'specific CBT components offered in which sequence or combination produce what changes in what outcome domains' (Durlak *et al.*, 1991).

CHAPTER TWO

Cognitive behaviour therapy with children and young people

▶ Cognitive behaviour therapy with children under 12 years of age

Cognitive behaviour therapy (CBT) requires an ability to systematically identify, challenge and generate alternative ways of thinking. The process involves a degree of cognitive maturity and sophistication, and requires an ability to engage in abstract tasks such as viewing events from different perspectives or generating alternative attributions. The degree to which young children have the required level of cognitive maturity to be able to 'think about thinking' has been the subject of debate.

Although this debate continues, CBT is often used with young children. A review of 101 CBT intervention studies found that 79% included children under the age of 10 years (Durlak *et al.*, 1995). CBT has been successfully used with children under the age of 7 years presenting with a range of problems, including encopresis (Ronen, 1993), enuresis (Ronen *et al.*, 1995), school refusal (King *et al.*, 1998), abdominal pain (Sanders *et al.*, 1994), generalized anxiety disorders (Dadds *et al.*, 1997; Silverman *et al.*, 1999a), phobias (Silverman *et al.*, 1999b), sexual abuse (Cohen and Mannarino, 1996; Deblinger *et al.*, 1990) and preschool behaviour problems (Douglas, 1998).

Although CBT has been used with young children, those under the age of 9 years have been found to benefit less than older children. A meta-analysis of cognitive behaviour therapy with children under the age of 13 years concluded that although children of all ages benefited from CBT, younger children benefited less (Durlak *et al.*, 1991). However, whether younger children were not sufficiently cognitively mature to engage with the tasks of CBT or whether the intervention was not pitched at the right level is unclear. Few studies have reported how interventions have been modified for younger children. Adapting and matching the concepts and techniques of CBT to the developmental level of the child may help to overcome some of the perceived developmental issues (Ronen, 1992).

Although CBT can be sophisticated and complex, many of the tasks require an ability to reason effectively about concrete matters and issues rather than abstract conceptual thinking (Harrington *et al.*, 1998). The concrete operational stage of cognitive development that is typically acquired during the middle years (around 7–12 years of age) is sufficient for many of the basic tasks of cognitive behavioural therapy (Verduyn, 2000). However, material does need to be pitched at the appropriate level. More concrete techniques with clear and simple instructions are useful for most younger children, whereas adolescents can usually engage in more sophisticated processes, such as identifying dysfunctional assumptions and cognitive restructuring.

The challenge when working with younger children is how to translate abstract concepts into simple, concrete, understandable examples and metaphors from the child's everyday life. CBT should be fun, interesting and engaging, with materials and concepts presented at an age-appropriate level (Young and Brown, 1996). For example, Ronen (1992) provided ideas about how the concepts of automatic thoughts (i.e. 'doing something without thinking about it') and mediated thoughts (i.e. 'a command or order that the brain sends to the body') were conveyed to children through play. Mediated thoughts were described in a game of soldiers as the commander (brain) sending orders to their soldiers (your body). Similarly, automatic thoughts were explained during a painting session about a river, where the river could either wander wherever it chose (automatic thoughts) or the flow could be changed and made to go where the child wanted (mediated thoughts).

Metaphors can help by providing ways in which abstract concepts can be described and understood in concrete terms. For example, an aggressive child could be helped to think about his/her anger as a volcano that builds up and erupts. Thinking in this way may help the child to explore how he/she can stop the volcano blowing its top. Similarly, the metaphor of a tape playing in the child's head can be used to describe automatic thoughts, or a videotape can be used to help the child to understand intrusive images. Metaphors such as these can then lead to the development of self-control strategies. The child may be helped to explore how his/her automatic thoughts or intrusive images can be controlled by turning off his/her tape.

The use of imagery has been reported with children as young as 5 years of age, in whom the method of emotive imagery developed by Lazarus and Abramovitz (1962) has been used to help to overcome darkness phobias (Jackson and King, 1981; King *et al.*, 1998). Positive coping images are used as a way to facilitate a strong positive affect, which is antagonistic to unpleasant emotional reactions such as anxiety or anger. Thus Jackson and King (1981) used the image of the comic character Batman to help a young boy to overcome his fear of the dark. Similarly, imagery could be used with older children where, for example, a comic image such as a person wearing a silly hat might help to diffuse angry feelings arising from teasing. In order to be effective, positive coping images need to be tailored to the age of the child and built upon his/her existing interests and fantasies (Rosenstiel and Scott, 1977).

- ■ Children at least 7 years of age will be able to engage in CBT.
- ■ The intervention needs to be pitched to the cognitive developmental level of the child.
- ■ The challenge for the practitioner is to translate abstract concepts into simple, concrete everyday examples to which children can relate.

▶ Assessing the basic skills required to engage in cognitive behaviour therapy

The core cognitive skills required to engage in cognitive behaviour therapy have not been defined. At a basic level, children need to be able to access and communicate their thoughts. In addition, Doherr *et al.* (1999) identified a further three key tasks, namely an ability to generate alternative attributions about events, an awareness of different emotions, and an ability to connect thoughts and feelings in different situations.

■ Accessing and communicating thoughts

Direct questioning: describe what you are thinking

Interviewing can provide a rich source of information about the child's thoughts and self-talk (Hughes, 1988). It has been suggested that, during an interview, children as young as 3 years of age can provide information about their thoughts (Hughes, 1988). At the simplest level this can be determined by asking a child to describe 'what you are thinking' or 'what thoughts were running through your head when you first met me'. Some children will be able to identify and articulate a range of thoughts relating to the cognitive triad. They may report thoughts relating to the perception of themselves (e.g. 'I feel silly talking with you', 'you must think I'm an idiot to get upset by these things'), of the world as unfair (e.g. 'I had to miss football training to come here', 'it's my mum who has got the problem. Talk with her, not me') or the future (e.g. 'I don't think there is any point me being here. It's not going to make any difference').

However, a number of children will respond to such direct questioning with comments such as 'I don't know' or 'I wasn't thinking about anything'. This does not necessarily imply that the child cannot access his/her thoughts, but rather it suggests the need to try an alternative, indirect approach.

Indirect approach: describe a recent difficult situation

Younger children will probably find it easier to think about a recent difficult situation. Help them to describe it, or draw a picture about it, and as they talk or draw, note whether they are able to provide both a description of what happened and some of their thoughts/attributions about the event. Prompting the children to express their thoughts at specific times, such as prior to, during or immediately after an event, can provide a useful structure for helping to identify their self-talk (Kendall and Chansky, 1991). At other times, careful probing and prompting during the interview may help the child to gain access to their thoughts, as illustrated in the example below.

Mike, aged 7 years, had recently hit a child at school, resulting in him and his parents having to meet with the headteacher. The incident was discussed during our meeting and the account was as follows:

CLINICIAN: Mike, can you tell me about that fight you had at school?

MIKE: Luke started it. He pushed me so I hit him. I got into trouble and that's it.

CLINICIAN: How did Luke start it?

MIKE: He called me names.

CLINICIAN: Does he often call you names?

MIKE: No.

CLINICIAN: Why do you think he called you names?

MIKE: Don't know. I suppose he hates me.

CLINICIAN: Is it just you or are there other people at school he hates?

MIKE: No, just me. He likes everyone else.

CLINICIAN: Does Luke fight with other people?

MIKE: Yes. He's always fighting.

CLINICIAN: Does he like the other people he fights with?

MIKE: I don't know. I think it's just me he hates.

CLINICIAN: What do you think will happen next time you see Luke?

MIKE: He'll hit me. That's why I'm going to hit him first.

This very brief discussion started to show how Mike had access to his thoughts. He perceived himself to be hated and was predicting that Luke was going to hit him again.

What might someone else be thinking?

Younger children may have difficulty accessing and describing their own cognitions, but may be able to describe what someone else is thinking (Kane and Kendall, 1989). Puppets and games can be used to create and role play the child's difficult situation, and in the course of play the child can be asked to show or say what the puppets might be thinking.

An alternative, more structured approach is to provide the child with a set of possible options from which he/she can choose. This forms the basis of the Attributional Style Questionnaire (Fielstein *et al.*, 1985), where the child is presented with 12 vignettes and asked to select which of four possible outcomes (e.g. perceived lack of skill, effort, luck or complexity of task) has caused the event. Although this does not provide information about the child's own specific cognitions, it does provide a useful insight into how the child construes his or her world.

Thought bubbles

An alternative non-verbal approach is to provide the child with cartoons or pictures and to ask him/her to suggest what the people/characters may be thinking. This approach has been advocated by Kendall and Chansky (1991), and has been used in the Coping Cat programme for treating anxiety (Kendall, 1992). For example, in the Coping Cat programme the child is asked to suggest what an ice skater or a child cooking a sausage on a barbecue might be thinking.

This approach can be simply adapted by the clinician depending on the materials that they have available. For example, a child could be asked to suggest what the cat and mouse may be thinking about in the following picture.

■ **Generating alternative attributions**

Hypothetical situations

Doherr *et al.* (1999) have devised a series of simple hypothetical situations to assess whether children are able to identify alternative attributions for events. The child is presented with a series of scenarios, some of which are modelled on and adapted from those used by Greenberg and Padesky (1995). For example, 'a child in a playground shouts "hello" at his friend, but his friend just runs past'. The child is then asked to think of as many different explanations as he/she can for what has happened.

Approaches such as this have also been used to explore problem-solving skills. The Preschool Interpersonal Problem-Solving Inventory provides a set of pictorial vignettes, and the child is asked to generate as many solutions as possible to the dilemma (Spivack and Shure, 1974). Similarly, means end thinking can be assessed by using the Means Ends Problem-Solving Inventory (Spivack *et al.*, 1976). The start and ending of a story are provided, and the child is asked to identify as many ways as possible in which the ending could be achieved.

Generative cartoons

The child can be given a series of pictures or cartoons and then be asked to draw or write as many ideas as he/she can about what one of the characters may be thinking. In the following picture the child could be asked to complete the thought bubbles by drawing or writing what the person with the parcel may be thinking.

Puppets and play

A difficult situation can be acted out, and during the course of play the child can be encouraged to suggest what each of the other puppets or toys may think about what has happened. The age of the child needs to be considered since, as Salmon and Bryant (2002) highlight, pre-school children experience difficulties if they are asked to use a doll or puppet to represent themselves. They have difficulties understanding that the doll/puppet can be both an object (toy) and a symbol (representation of themselves).

■ **Awareness of emotions**

A core element of many cognitive behavioural therapy programmes is affective education designed to help children to become aware of and distinguish between different feelings. In order to participate in such a process, children need to be able to access their feelings and provide a description of them. However, the extent to which this is a prerequisite for CBT or an awareness that develops during CBT is unclear.

There are many different materials available to help children to identify and express their own emotions through play, games and drawing (see, for example, Hobday and Ollier, 1998; Sunderland and Engleheart, 1993). Young children may not necessarily be able to provide a verbal description of their feelings, but they may be able to draw them. Similarly, they may only talk about one feeling, such as being angry, although on careful questioning it might emerge that there is an 'angry angry', a 'sad angry' or a 'scared angry'.

Quizzes and games can be used to assess whether the child can identify the feelings of another person. Children can be given pictures of people in different emotional states and asked to identify what they might be feeling from a list of emotions. Similarly, the clinician could role play different emotions and ask the child to suggest a name for how they are feeling.

■ **Thoughts, feelings and events**

Once again the use of puzzles and quizzes will allow you to determine whether the child is able to demonstrate an awareness of different emotions in different situations. For example, the child could be provided with or generate a set of feeling cards (e.g. frightened, happy, angry, etc.) and be asked to place the card that best describes how he/she feels about various situations (e.g. first day at school, playing with my best friend, being told off, etc.). Similarly, the task could involve matching feelings with a range of different thoughts (e.g. 'I think I am going to get this wrong', 'I think I played well in this game', 'I think my friends will tease me'). Alternatively, this task could be acted out using puppets, where the child has to describe how his or her puppet might feel in various situations (e.g. if they were teased or if they were invited to their friend's birthday party).

To engage in CBT, children have to be able to undertake tasks such as:

■ accessing and communicating their thoughts;

■ generating alternative attributions for events;

■ being aware of different emotions;

■ linking thoughts, feelings and events.

These can be assessed in a variety of age-appropriate ways by using games, quizzes, puppets, drawing and cartoons.

▶ Cognitive behaviour therapy with adolescents

The use of CBT with adolescents requires an understanding of the developmental issues that may impact upon the process. Belsher and Wilkes (1994) identified a number of issues that need to be considered.

Acknowledge the adolescent's self-centredness

Adolescents often present as self-centred and have difficulty seeing and accepting the views of others. It is often useful to acknowledge and accept this position by pursuing questions which aim to clarify and understand the adolescent's views, rather than directly challenging his or her egocentricity. Adopting such a therapeutic stance conveys a positive message to the adolescent that his or her views are being heard and respected. They are being seen as important, with their own interesting and unique perceptions which the therapist is keen to understand. Failing to acknowledge the adolescent's egocentricity may result in the development of an oppositional stance whereby the adolescent feels under increasing pressure to argue and defend his or her views.

The adolescent's sense of self-determination can be further enhanced by regularly presenting him/her with choices and options during the course of CBT. Belsher and Wilkes (1994) suggest that adolescents should be presented with two or three versions of a similar task from which they could choose. For example, the clinician could suggest that thought monitoring could be achieved by completing a structured record sheet, more informally by keeping a private thought diary, or by talking into a tape recorder when 'hot thoughts' are noticed. The role of the clinician is that of an option provider, with the adolescent deciding which method to pursue.

Promote collaboration

CBT is a collaborative process, although children and adolescents are often in a 'one-down' position relative to the adult clinician. The power and status differential between young people and the clinician needs to be recognized and a conscious effort must be made to promote a more equal relationship.

The clinician needs to convey a sense of willingness to work with the adolescent to help him/her to overcome the problems which he/she identifies as important. The clinician is an educator and facilitator, who provides a framework within which the young person can explore, understand and identify new ways of thinking and behaving. The collaborative process encourages the young person to think through his or her problems and difficulties and to discover possible solutions. The young person therefore has a key role in target setting and decision making, and the collaborative approach can be further enhanced by the clinician acting as an advocate and conveying the adolescent's views to other significant authority figures.

Promote objectivity

Although the clinician may at times act as an advocate for the young person, it is important that he or she maintains an objective stance. Adolescents are self-centred, often hold very strong views and find it difficult to consider others' perspectives. This may result in the young person placing the clinician under pressure to agree with or endorse his/her subjective view.

The clinician needs to remain objective and promote a model of collaborative empiricism whereby the young person is encouraged to test his or her own views and to look for evidence that would support or challenge them. The clinician provides the structure within which the young person tests and evaluates his or her own assumptions, beliefs and thoughts. Given that cognitive distortions underpin many psychological problems, the adolescent may process the outcome of his/her test in a biased way. This can be directly addressed during clinical sessions by helping the young person to generate and explore alternative explanations which could again be tested.

Use Socratic questions

Adolescents and children are less familiar with processes that encourage their active participation and expression of beliefs and ideas. They may feel that their views are unimportant or 'wrong' and expect, as occurs in many aspects of their life, to be told what they should do. Socratic questioning is a useful way of overcoming this obstacle where, by a series of questions, the young person is helped to explore, reassess and challenge his or her beliefs.

Questioning is very direct and specific, and often relates to concrete events. Thus instead of asking a general question such as 'What happened at school yesterday?', the young person might be invited to respond to the question 'What did you think Mike was going to do when he came up to you in the playground after lunch?'.

Adolescents can be encouraged to express their ideas by prefixing questions with short statements such as 'There are probably many different ways we could deal with this . . . what would you do?'. The idea that some situations may not have answers can be conveyed by statements such as 'I can't think of anything . . . do you have any ideas?'. Reflecting back statements made by the young person helps to reinforce your interest in them, but it also allows distortions and inconsistencies to be challenged. For example, 'Can I check that I have understood what you said? You told me that you haven't got any friends, but that Melanie has invited you to a sleepover. Isn't Melanie your friend?'.

Challenge dichotomous thinking

'All-or-nothing' thinking is common in adolescents, and is often reflected in the dramatic oscillation that may be encountered from session to session. On one occasion an adolescent may present as depressed or anxious, yet by the next session he/she may be happy or relaxed. These dramatic swings often leave clinicians feeling confused and unsure about the need to continue with CBT. Although significant and lasting improvements can be achieved with children and young people in a comparatively small number of sessions, there are times when the apparent recovery is short-lived and is more a reflection of the adolescent's dichotomous thinking.

Rating scales are a useful way of challenging dichotomous thinking, and they help the adolescent to recognize that there is a whole range of stages between their two extreme anchor points. This may require some degree of education, and it could involve the adolescent rating or ordering a series of events along a particular dimension. Scales can be used to rate the intensity of feelings, belief in thoughts, degree of responsibility or blame.

Finally, Belsher and Wilkes (1994) highlight the importance of the language used by the clinician. Asking what would be 'good' or 'bad' suggests a dichotomous categorization, whereas using the terms 'better' or 'worse' conveys the impression of a graded continuum.

Involve other significant people

Adolescents operate within a complex social system involving the significant influences of families/carers, friends and schools. It is important to recognize and involve these as appropriate, since adolescents are often unable to make decisions about things that affect them. For example, adolescents who are practising anger management strategies at school may need their class teacher to allow them to leave the classroom when they become angry. Similarly, involving other significant figures (e.g. parents, siblings or friends) in sessions can provide a different perspective which can help young people to test and re-evaluate their own cognitions.

> - Acknowledge the adolescent's self-centredness.
> - Promote collaboration.
> - Promote objectivity.
> - Use Socratic questions.
> - Challenge dichotomous thinking.
> - Involve other significant people.

▶ Common problems when undertaking cognitive behaviour therapy with children and adolescents

Non-communicating children

The process of CBT with children is typically less didactic than that with adults, and children often adopt a more passive listening role during clinical sessions. Although this may require greater input from the clinician, it does not necessarily imply that CBT is ineffective. Indeed, one of the key issues in working with children is the need to adapt materials so that they are accessible to the child. In these situations, greater use of non-verbal materials is helpful, and children will often vocalize their thoughts and feelings while playing or drawing. Similarly, the use of media such as blackboards and flip charts can attract the child's interest and result in increased participation.

At other times, despite the creative use of materials, children may remain silent throughout sessions and respond with vague, non-committal answers to any probes and questions. On these occasions it might be useful to employ a more rhetorical approach whereby you guess aloud what the young person might reply to your questions. Similarly, if the young person is reluctant to talk about him- or herself, then discussing the similar problems of a third party, or acting them out through the use of puppets or play, can often result in more engagement. Finally, it may be useful to change the setting, so rather than sitting in the clinic, try going for a coffee or a walk and see if the young person then becomes more communicative.

Reluctant customers

Children do not typically refer themselves for psychological help, but are usually brought to the clinician by concerned carers and professionals. The children themselves may not share these concerns or indeed perceive any particular problems that require help.

A core feature of CBT is the collaborative nature of the intervention, and if the child is unable to identify any goals or changes that they would like to make, then the use of CBT should be questioned. However, this requires careful exploration, since the child's inability to identify possible goals may be a result of his or her experience (i.e. 'this is the way it has always been and always will be'). Helping the child to explore alternative, realistic possibilities may help him/her to recognize that his/her situation could be different. Similarly, a lack of motivation, as found for example with depressed children, may result in the expression of reluctance and hopelessness. In these cases, motivational interviewing may be helpful in securing the young person's commitment to at least experimenting with CBT (Miller and Rollnick, 1991). Motivational interviewing utilizes basic counselling techniques (e.g. empathy, positive regard, active listening) and cognitive behavioural interventions (e.g. positive restructuring) to increase a person's commitment to change. The child is encouraged to express his or her own views and perceptions of events while the clinician selectively listens for and reinforces possible signs of motivation. These are then reflected back to the young person.

No responsibility for securing change

Children and young people may identify difficulties and identify targets for change, but may not view themselves as responsible for achieving them. Sometimes this will be appropriate, but at other times difficulties may be attributed to organic factors (e.g. 'this is me, I was born like this') or external factors that are not perceived as being within the individual's ability to change. For example, a young person who is regularly in trouble at school may attribute this externally as being unfairly picked on by teachers (e.g. 'if the teachers didn't pick on me, then I wouldn't be in trouble'). Whether this is really the case, or whether it is a reflection of distorted or biased views, needs to be assessed. However, the young person needs to be prepared at least to explore his/her personal contribution to these events in order to engage in CBT.

Involving parents

There is increasing evidence to suggest that involving parents in CBT with children may produce additional benefits (Barrett et al., 1996; King et al., 1998; Toren et al., 2000). The specific role of parents in CBT programmes has varied, and has included those of facilitator, co-therapist and client. The main role of the facilitator is to aid transfer of skills from clinical sessions to the home environment. Parents may contribute to the assessment of difficult situations and encourage and allow their child to practise new skills and tasks at home. The co-therapist has more of an active role in which the parent might prompt, monitor and review their child's use of cognitive skills. Parents are encouraged to reinforce their child and to work with them in planning and addressing problems. In both cases the child remains the focus of the intervention, with the parents working towards reducing their child's psychological distress.

Finally, parents can be involved as clients in their own right, learning new skills (e.g. behaviour management) or how to cope with their own problems (e.g. managing anxiety). This model has been advocated by Barrett (1998), who describes a systemic model to empower parents and children to form an 'expert team'. Parents receive training in behaviour management, how to deal with their own emotional upsets, and communication and problem-solving skills. Similarly, Cobham, Dadds and Spence (1998) describe an intervention that incorporates both child-focused CBT to treat child anxiety and a programme designed to reduce parental anxiety. Parents are taught to recognise the effect of their own behaviour on the development and maintenance of their child's problems and how to address their own anxiety.

The parents' role in the intervention, and thus the extent and nature of their involvement in the programme, needs to be clarified and agreed at the outset.

Should there be collaboration with the child or their parent/carer?

A more fundamental issue arising from the involvement of parents relates to the process of collaboration and whether the child or their parent is seen as the primary client. This can be a source of tension, since children may identify different goals and targets to their parents, raising the question of whose agenda should be addressed. Pursuing the parent's or adult's agenda raises ethical issues with regard to whether their goals are designed to secure conformity or concerned with furthering the best interests of the child (Royal College of Psychiatry, 1997).

The clinician needs to manage these different perspectives by listening and expressing interest in each while maintaining a detached, objective and impartial position. Repeatedly clarifying the overall goal of therapy, namely to reduce the child's or adolescent's psychological distress, helps to maintain the focus while highlighting the fact that this goal can often be achieved in a number of ways. Initially responding to the child's or adolescent's agenda conveys a strong message to the young person that his/her views are important and that they have a key role in determining change. This sense of self-determination can be further enhanced by focusing on realistic and achievable targets that result in some degree of rapid success. Finally, reviewing progress provides an opportunity to monitor change, reassess the goals of the child and his/her parents and identify and agree on the next target. This process is helpful and often demonstrates that positive changes arising from pursuing the child's agenda also have positive effects on the adult goals.

On other occasions, the child and his/her parents can be helped by the clinician to agree on a common focus. The protocol for treating obsessive-compulsive disorder (OCD) developed by March et al. (1994) provides an example of how the child and his or her parents can work together to overcome the child's obsessions. The child is encouraged to give his or her OCD a nasty name and to learn how to boss back obsessional urges. The parents are helped to distinguish between OCD and their child by externalizing OCD as an illness that they can help their child to overcome.

Significant family dysfunction

The dynamics within a family are complex and can result in individual children being inappropriately perceived as responsible for all of the family's difficulties. In such situations, individual CBT would not be appropriate if it did not address the wider family issues. Similarly, if the child's perceived cognitive deficits or distortions reflect limited parental capabilities or maladaptive parental views, then individual CBT would be inappropriate and unlikely to be effective (Kaplan *et al.*, 1995). The clinician needs to undertake a thorough assessment in order to determine whether the child's comments that his/her parents are 'always putting me down' represent a cognitive distortion or an accurate reflection of a dysfunctional family. Determining this will indicate whether individual CBT or a more systemic approach is indicated.

Difficulty in accessing thoughts

Children and young people often find it difficult to identify and vocalize their thoughts, particularly in response to direct questions. However, careful listening will reveal that beliefs, assumptions and appraisals are often evident as they talk. At these times it is often useful for the clinician to adopt the role of the 'thought catcher' described by Turk (1998), identifying important cognitions when they occur and bringing them to the attention of the young person. The clinician may stop the dialogue and bring the young person's attention to the cognitions they have just verbalized, or alternatively they may be held and summarized at a suitable time. For example, the clinician may listen to a child's description of a recent 'hot' situation and then summarize the key feelings and associated thoughts that they identified.

Children and young people often confuse thoughts and feelings, which led Belsher and Wilkes (1994) to highlight the need to 'chase the effect'. The authors suggest that during clinical sessions particular attention should be paid to changes in emotion, which are fed back to the child in order to identify the associated cognitions (e.g. 'you seem to be thinking about something that is making you angry'). Often children will require further help to discover their cognitions, and the clinician can either pursue Socratic questioning or provide a list of possible suggestions which the young person can reject or agree with. By a process of observation and careful questioning the child can discover and vocalize the cognitions underlying their emotions.

Failure to undertake home-based assignments

CBT is an active process that typically involves the gathering of information outside clinical sessions. Although some children and adolescents are interested and keen to undertake home-based monitoring, others are unwilling to do so and repeatedly fail to return with any material. This issue needs to be discussed openly with the young person, the importance of the assignments explained and the extent of what can realistically be undertaken, if anything, agreed. Terminology is important, and it is useful to avoid calling out-of-session assignments or experiments 'homework', which may be viewed negatively. Identifying an appropriate way of undertaking the task is also important. For example, children may be reluctant to write a thought diary but may be more interested in keeping a record on their computer. Similarly, some young people may be more motivated to email their thoughts to you, while others may prefer to talk into a tape recorder.

Completing home-based assignments is not a prerequisite for undertaking CBT. The experiences, thoughts and feelings of those children who are unable to keep records can still be assessed during clinical sessions. They can be asked to talk you through a recent difficult situation, and the clinician can probe and explore the thoughts and feelings that accompanied the event.

Limited cognitive ability/verbal skills

A basic level of cognitive, memory and verbal skills is required to engage in CBT, and consequently children with significant developmental issues may not be able to engage in the process directly. However, it needs to be established whether this is due to the child's limited cognitive abilities or to cognitive tasks not being pitched at the right level to allow the child to access them.

Presenting information more visually, using simpler language and presenting abstract concepts in more concrete ways can make it easier for people with learning disabilities to engage in CBT (Whitaker, 2001). Memory problems can be overcome by the use of visual cues and prompts. For example, a child who is learning to use traffic lights as a way of problem solving (red, stop and think; amber, plan; green, try it out) can be reminded to use this system at school by wrapping coloured strips around their pen. Similarly, tasks can be simplified with fewer decision points so that a child can be helped to 'bail out' of (i.e. walk away from) situations in which they might lose their temper, rather than learning a more complex set of responses.

Brief interventions

Children and adolescents often adopt a short-term problem-focused perspective. They are typically interested in addressing immediate pressing problems rather than embarking on longer-term work. Consequently, with children and young people there is a greater emphasis on facilitating and developing cognitive coping skills rather than addressing underlying schemas or beliefs.

Typically there is less focus on abstract complexities, such as understanding the subtle nuances of different types of cognitive distortions. Instead, children and adolescents are often keen to understand their difficulties within a cognitive framework and to learn more appropriate cognitive and behavioural skills to enable them to cope with them. This predominant focus on real-time problems often results in CBT with children being undertaken in far fewer sessions than with adults. Although a number of CBT interventions for children identify 12–16 session programmes, clinical experience suggests that many interventions are considerably shorter than this. Significant change can be achieved in six or even fewer sessions, resulting in many clinicians feeling confused or questioning whether CBT has in fact been undertaken. This confusion is understandable and relates to the question posed at the end of Chapter 1 concerning what CBT with children entails. The cognitive focus of many CBT interventions is extremely limited, often being confined to the development of one particular cognitive strategy. Until the core effective elements have been defined, clinicians will continue to question their practice.

Common problems encountered when undertaking CBT with children and adolescents include the following:

- non-communicating children;
- 'reluctant customers';
- no responsibility for securing change;
- identifying the role of the parent;
- significant family dysfunction;
- establishing with whom collaboration should occur;
- difficulty in accessing thoughts;
- failure to undertake home-based assignments;
- limited cognitive/verbal skills;
- brief interventions.

CHAPTER THREE

Think good – feel good: an overview of materials

Think Good – Feel Good is a collection of materials that have adapted the concepts and strategies of CBT for use with children and adolescents. Through three main characters, the Thought Tracker, Feeling Finder and Go Getter, children and young people are helped to understand the cognitive behavioural framework, to explore and test their cognitions and to learn alternative cognitive and behavioural skills. The characters may be of more interest to younger children, who may find it easier to think about and describe thoughts and feelings through a third party. For adolescents it may be appropriate to focus more on the materials and less on the characters.

Think Good – Feel Good is not intended to be delivered systematically as a package. It does not represent a standardized 10-session course, nor is it a comprehensive CBT programme. Instead, it provides a range of materials that can be used flexibly depending on the needs of the child and the nature of their difficulties. The materials provide examples of how the concepts of CBT can be conveyed in an enjoyable, simple and understandable way.

Think Good – Feel Good provides educational materials and accompanying exercises for each of the following topics:

1. introduction to CBT;
2. automatic thoughts;
3. common cognitive distortions;
4. cognitive restructuring and balanced thinking;
5. core beliefs;
6. developing new cognitive skills;
7. identifying feelings;
8. strategies for controlling unpleasant feelings;
9. ideas for changing behaviour;
10. approaches to problem solving.

Each topic has an explanatory section that provides a concrete and understandable summary of the key issues. Illustrations and practical examples provide a way of relating the materials to issues and problems with which the young person may be familiar. The explanatory section can be photocopied and used as a handout, or it can be used to structure the clinical session. The clinician can then emphasize and focus on those issues that are most relevant for the child.

A series of worksheets accompany each section, to help the child to apply the information to his or her own particular difficulties. The worksheets vary in complexity, those marked with a smiling face being more appropriate for younger children. The worksheets provide examples of how the concepts can be conveyed, and are intended to be used flexibly and adapted by the clinician.

► **Thoughts, feelings and what you do**

Summary

This section provides an introduction to cognitive behaviour therapy and explains the link between thoughts, feelings and behaviour. Different types of thoughts (automatic and core beliefs) are explained, the role of assumptions is highlighted, and the effects of positive and negative thoughts on feelings and behaviour are described. The negative trap, whereby negative thoughts produce unpleasant feelings that limit or restrict behaviour, is also identified.

- ■ Psycho-education.
- ■ Introduction to the core elements of thoughts, feelings and behaviour.

Worksheets

The *Magic Circle* and the *Negative Trap* introduce the child to the concept of thought monitoring and the link between thoughts, feelings and behaviour. The Magic Circle focuses on an enjoyable situation and teases out what the child thinks and what they do. In contrast, the Negative Trap explores difficult situations, as can be seen in this example involving 8-year-old Amy who became very anxious when going to school. During the interview her thoughts, feelings and what she did were identified and put together in the summary below.

My thoughts
'Have I got everything?'
'What have I forgotten?'
'My teacher will be cross'
'The others will laugh'
'I don't feel well'

Amy walks to school

What I do
Cry
Stand still
Won't go into class
Run out of school

My feelings
Scared/worried
Shaking
Sweating
Heart beating fast

Comparisons can be made between the Magic Circle and the Negative Trap to highlight the fact that thoughts produce different feelings and have helpful or unhelpful effects on behaviour. Finally, depending on the child, the feeling section could be subdivided into feelings (emotions) and body changes (physiological reactions). This may be particularly useful for those children who perceive their emotional reactions as signs of physical illness.

The *If/Then Quiz* is a way of discovering some of the assumptions that the child might make, while *What I Think, What I Do or How I Feel* is a puzzle that helps to distinguish between the three core elements of the CBT framework. Both can be adapted and modified for the individual child, with key themes that emerge during assessment being incorporated into questions that can be introduced into the quiz.

▶ Automatic thoughts

Summary

Automatic thoughts are explained by the metaphor of a tape playing in the child's head. The cognitive triad (thoughts about me, what I do and my future) is introduced and used to help to identify the different focus of their thoughts. The reasons why automatic thoughts seem so reasonable are explained, and the effects of positive and negative automatic thoughts on feelings and behaviour are explored. Finally, the need to identify 'hot' thoughts that produce strong emotional reactions is highlighted.

- Introduction to automatic thoughts and the cognitive triad.
- Thought monitoring and identification of common negative thoughts.

Worksheets

For older children, a *thought and feelings diary* provides a structure for recording 'Hot' Thoughts and linking these to emotional reactions. If home-based monitoring is not possible, then *'Hot' Thoughts* provides a way of identifying during a clinical session the common thoughts that the child may have about themselves, what they do and their future. Structured diaries and exercises can be useful for some children, whereas others will prefer a more flexible approach. Encouraging the child to make his or her own diary on his or her computer, to email hot thoughts to the clinician, to 'download his or her head' into a tape recorder or to simply 'catch' the occasional thought when it occurs are all possibilities.

For younger children, a series of *Thought Bubbles* relating to the cognitive triad are included. Children are encouraged to draw a picture or write down some of the nice or unpleasant thoughts that they have about themselves – nice thoughts about what they do or worrying thoughts about the future. Once again the bubbles can be adapted to pursue important themes identified by the clinician. If young children find it difficult to verbalize their thoughts, then the parents could be asked to suggest the types of thoughts that their child may have.

For those children who appear to experience persistent difficulty in accessing their thoughts, *What Are They Thinking?* may be helpful. The child is asked to suggest what two different characters in a picture may be thinking, or to generate two or three suggestions about what thoughts one character may have. This provides a way of assessing whether the child is able to identify and verbalize cognitions, and introduces them to the idea of describing thoughts.

▶ Thinking errors

Summary

Cognitive distortions are introduced as thinking errors which bias the way in which events are perceived. Cognitive distortions result in positive events being overlooked or their importance minimized. Six main types of errors are described. The 'downers' are those where negative events are focused on while anything positive is overlooked (selective abstraction, disqualifying the positive). 'Blowing things up' highlights how the importance attached to negative events is exaggerated (dichotomous thinking, magnification, over-generalization). 'Predicting failure' explains how bad things are expected to happen (arbitrary inference). 'Feeling thoughts' demonstrates how emotions take over and cloud thinking (emotional reasoning), while 'setting yourself up to fail' highlights how unachievable standards are often set (unrealistic expectations). Finally, 'blame me' identifies how responsibility for the negative events that happen is automatically assumed (personalization).

> ■ Identification of types of cognitive distortions.
> ■ Thought monitoring and identification of common cognitive distortions.

Worksheets

Identifying Thinking Errors is designed to help the child to capture negative thoughts and to identify the common types of cognitive distortions that they make. Once again the process for achieving this can be adapted to the child, and if out-of-session assignments are not possible, it can be undertaken as part of a clinical session. The idea of scaling is introduced, and the child is encouraged both to identify and to rate the extent to which he or she believe his/her negative thoughts. The diary is completed the following day when the thoughts are re-examined, thinking errors are identified, and their belief in the thought is rated again. The use of ratings begins to challenge the dichotomous thinking of many young people and provides a way of demonstrating that beliefs can change over time.

What Thinking Errors Do You Make? is a short assessment covering the six types of distortions identified in the handout. It provides a brief way for the young person to assess which types of cognitive distortions he or she makes, and which are his or her most common types.

▶ Balanced thinking

Summary

The young person is introduced to a process of checking and testing negative thoughts. This is designed to ensure that he/she has looked for all of the evidence and that his or her thoughts are balanced and not distorted. The process involves concrete steps of checking for evidence that supports and evidence that disproves the thoughts, gaining the perspective of another person, and checking for thinking errors. This leads to the final step of cognitive restructuring where, on the basis of all of the evidence, the young person identifies an alternative and more balanced thought.

> ■ Cognitive evaluation.
> ■ Thought testing.
> ■ Cognitive restructuring.
> ■ Balanced thinking.

Worksheets

Looking for Evidence is designed to help the child to become familiar with the thought-checking process. 'Hot' thoughts are identified and then assessed in order to determine supportive evidence, evidence that disproves them, what someone else would say, what they would say to someone else if they had this thought, and whether they are making any thinking errors. Rating the strength of belief before and after testing provides an objective means of demonstrating that negative automatic thoughts can become less troublesome if they are challenged.

Balanced Thinking takes the process of thought challenging to the final stage of cognitive restructuring. On the basis of all of the evidence, the young person identifies a more balanced and less biased thought.

▶ Core beliefs

Summary

The concepts of core beliefs are introduced, and the downward arrow 'So What?' technique is used to identify them. A process for testing core beliefs by actively looking for evidence that disproves them is described. The notion of core beliefs being strong and resistant to challenge is introduced, and the need to discuss and talk with someone else is advocated.

- ■ Identification of core beliefs.
- ■ Challenging and testing core beliefs.

Worksheets

Identifying Core Beliefs is an exercise in which the child uses the downward arrow 'So What?' technique to discover their core beliefs (Burns, 1980). After each statement, the child is asked 'So what? If this were true, what does this mean about you?' until the core belief is identified. Greenberger and Padesky (1995) highlight the fact that core beliefs appear as absolute statements such as 'I am/have . . .', 'others are . . .', etc.

Once the core beliefs have been identified, *Challenging Core Beliefs* can be used to test the validity of the belief. This is achieved by setting up an experiment to look for any evidence, no matter how small, which would suggest that the core belief is not always 100% true. Finally, *Common Beliefs* provides a means of assessing how strongly the child identifies with a set of 15 beliefs. Using the *Thought Thermometer*, the child rates how strongly they agree with each statement. This provides the clinician with an insight into the child's beliefs that can be used to help the child to discover why the same difficulties keep re-occurring or why they end up in the same negative traps.

▶ Controlling your thoughts

Summary

This section takes the young person through a variety of different ideas and strategies that can be used to manage dysfunctional and negative thoughts. Strategies for helping the young person to redirect and divert attention away from negative cognitions and physiological symptoms (e.g. distraction, absorbing activities) are described. Ideas for stopping (thought stopping) or turning down the volume (imagery) of their negative thoughts are provided. More balanced and helpful thoughts are promoted through strategies that develop positive or coping self-talk. Finally, the child is encouraged to experiment and test their predictions to see whether their thoughts and assumptions are true.

- Behavioural experiments.
- Distraction.
- Positive diaries.
- Positive self-talk.
- Coping self-talk.
- Thought stopping.

Worksheets

Test your Thoughts and Beliefs uses the process of guided discovery to help the young person to design an experiment to test the validity of his/her common thoughts and beliefs. Comparing predictions with the outcome of the experiment helps to identify, challenge and reduce the potency of distorted thoughts.

Thought Stopping provides a simple way of snapping an elastic band to help the child to stop listening to his/her negative thoughts and refocus his/her attention. *Turn the Tape Off* is an imaginative exercise that builds on the metaphor of thoughts being like a tape playing in the child's head. The child is helped to visualize the tape recorder in his/her head and then to imagine turning it off. For younger children, the *Worry Safe* provides a practical way of thought stopping. The child makes his/her own 'safe' out of a box in which he/she can deposit his or her worries. When worries arise, the child is encouraged to write or draw them and then to lock them away in his or her safe. The safe can be 'unlocked' with the therapist or the children's parents, and can be a useful way of discovering the nature and extent of the child's worries. The *Thought Challenger* takes thought stopping a stage further by stopping common negative thoughts and replacing them with more balanced cognitions.

The development of more balanced cognitions is promoted through three exercises. *Looking for the Positive* encourages children or their parents to actively seek the positive things that happen each day. This can be particularly useful for those children or parents who are overly focused on the child's failings or the things that are not right. *Positive Self-Talk* builds on this theme and helps children to find and acknowledge what they have achieved rather than areas in which they have failed. Instead of looking for what has yet to be achieved, the child is encouraged to find and praise his or her success. Finally, *Coping Self-Talk* helps the child to identify the thoughts that make him or her feel unpleasant and to replace these with coping self-talk which helps him or her to be successful and feel more relaxed and less anxious.

Practise Being Successful is another imaginative exercise designed to help the child to face challenges or difficult situations in a more positive way. The child imagines a challenge in as much detail as possible, but this time imagines him- or herself coping and being successful.

▶ How you feel

Summary

This section focuses on affective education and aims to increase awareness of different feelings and describes the common unpleasant emotions of stress, depression and anger. The relationship between feelings, thoughts and behaviour is highlighted.

- Affective education.
- Affective monitoring.

Worksheets

A number of different feelings can be introduced to the child through the *Feeling Finder Word Search*. After the child has found the different feelings in the puzzle, he or she can be asked to identify which of his/her are their most common feelings. An alternative approach for younger children to is to ask them to draw *'My Feelings'* on an outline of a person. The child is asked to identify and name his or her feelings, assign each of them a colour, and then to colour the person, showing how much of each feeling they have inside.

Older children may be helped to tune into their feelings through the *What Happens When I Feel . . .* worksheets. The child is asked to identify what their face and body look like and what they do when they feel angry, sad, anxious or happy. Once they have described the feeling, they are asked to rate how often they have this feeling, which can then lead onto a discussion exploring associated thoughts and activities. This simple exercise can be adapted to include other emotions. Those children who experience difficulty in describing their own emotions may be helped to identify the feelings of another person. Pictures of people showing different emotions can be collected from newspapers and the child is then asked to guess how these individuals are feeling. Similarly, the clinician could role play different emotional states which the child is then invited to guess.

Linking feelings to places and events can occur through *What Feeling Goes Where?* Children are given a set of feelings and places and asked to draw a line between the place and how they feel when they are there. An alternative is to ask children to generate a list of their own common feelings and the important places and events in their life. This forms the basis of *Feelings and Places*, in which the child chooses the feeling that best describes each situation. The connection between feelings and situations/events can be further highlighted by identifying the situations/events that produce the most pleasant/unpleasant feelings.

Finally, thoughts and activities that make the child feel good or unpleasant can be identified through the *Thoughts and Feelings* or *Activities and Feelings* worksheets.

▶ Controlling your feelings

Summary

Practical ways of controlling unpleasant feelings are identified. Muscular physical relaxation and quick relaxation exercises are described. The child is introduced to controlled breathing and the possible calming role of naturally occurring events such as physical exercise or absorbing activities. Relaxing imagery is developed by imagining a special calming place. Finally, the metaphor of a volcano is used to explain anger and the need to prevent the volcano from blowing its top.

- ▪ Affective management.
- ▪ Physical relaxation.
- ▪ Controlled breathing.
- ▪ Imaginal relaxation.
- ▪ Anger management.

Worksheets

Young children may be helped to reduce unpleasant feelings by using the *Feeling Strong Room*. This is similar to the Worry Safe, and involves the child making his or her own 'strong room' in which pictures or descriptions of unpleasant feelings can be deposited. Once again this can be reviewed with the clinician or the child's carers in order to identify the extent and nature of the child's unpleasant feelings. Filling in the thought bubbles of *My Relaxing Activities* may help to identify those activities that the child finds calming.

Younger children can be helped by *Learning to Relax*, where they are encouraged to tense and relax their muscles through a game of 'Simon Says'. Older children may find imagery more appealing, and a worksheet to enable them to identify and describe a picture of *My Relaxing Place* is included. When creating this image, it is important to describe the scene in as much detail as possible and to identify and build in a range of different sensations (e.g. sight, smell, touch, etc.).

The *Anger Volcano* can be used as a metaphor for children who experience aggressive outbursts. Children are helped to plot their own unique anger build-up by tuning into their thoughts, physiological reactions and behaviour as they progress from being calm through to an aggressive outburst. This is sequentially plotted on to their volcano, helping them to identify their anger build-up so that they can intervene at an earlier stage to prevent the volcano from blowing its top.

▶ Changing your behaviour

Summary

The way in which thoughts and feelings affect behaviour is explained. The need to become more active is emphasized, and increasing enjoyable activities is suggested as a first step. Rescheduling activities, breaking down challenges into smaller steps, graded exposure and response prevention are identified as ways in which the young person can regain control of his or her life.

- Activity monitoring.
- Activity rescheduling.
- Hierarchy development.
- Systematic desensitization.
- Response prevention.

Worksheets

A series of worksheets in which the child has to fill in thought bubbles by writing or drawing pictures can be used to identify *Things That Make Me Feel Good* or *Things That Make Me Feel Unpleasant*. Activities that are fun can be identified in a similar way through *Things I Would Like to Do*. Older children may prefer *Next Step Up the Ladder*, where enjoyable activities are identified and then placed in hierarchical order of difficulty. Starting with the easiest, the young person is systematically encouraged to become more active and to climb his or her ladder to success.

Feelings and activity can be monitored through an *Activity Diary* in which the child describes what he or she is doing and rates his/her mood for each hour throughout the day. This may identify particular patterns, with certain times or activities being more strongly associated with intense unpleasant feelings. This would lead to activity scheduling, where the child is encouraged to increase enjoyable activities or to explore different ways of timetabling his/her day in order to avoid times associated with strong unpleasant emotions.

The idea of breaking down tasks and challenges into smaller steps in order to increase the likelihood of success is explained through *Small Steps*. The child is helped to develop a staged hierarchy with the easier, less anxiety-provoking steps being successfully completed before progressing to the next stage. Small Steps forms part of the systematic desensitization programme, *Face Your Fears*, in which the child is helped to face and overcome fearful challenges. It is also used in the response prevention programme, *Dump Your Habits*, in which the child is helped to gain control of his/her behaviour and to stop his/her habits. Stopping long-standing habits is difficult, and the child may need someone else present to encourage and help them.

The need for self-reinforcement and reward for success is highlighted throughout this section. Children should be encouraged to find and celebrate their success, no matter how small it may be.

▶ Learning to solve problems

Summary

Three common reasons for problems are identified, namely acting without thinking, feelings taking over, or not being able to find alternative solutions. Ways of developing more effective problem-solving skills are explained, and a self-instructional traffic-light model of 'stop, plan and act' is suggested. Alternative and consequential thinking is highlighted, and ways in which new problem-solving skills can be prompted are explored. Finally, the need to practise new skills (both imaginative and *in vivo*) is highlighted.

- Alternative thinking.
- Consequential thinking.
- Self-instructional training.

Worksheets

Looking for Solutions is a thought bubble approach that can be used to enable younger children to think about different ways in which problems can be approached. Older children can be introduced to the idea of alternative thinking through *Identifying Possible Solutions*. The child is asked to generate as many different solutions to his or her problem as possible by ending each with the statement 'or'. Once alternative solutions have been identified, consequential thinking can be developed through *What are the Consequences of my Solutions?* The child is introduced to a problem-solving approach in which the positive and negative consequences of each solution are identified and assessed, to help them to find the best way of solving their problem.

A self-instructional approach to problem solving is used to help children to learn to *Stop, Plan and Go*. The image of a traffic light is developed to help the child to learn to stop, decide on an action plan and then implement it. Finally, *Talk Yourself Through It* provides another means by which children can learn to solve their problems. The child is helped to internalize successful problem solving by watching and listening to someone else coping successfully. Initially the child talks him- or herself through this plan out loud, but over time the volume is reduced and the plan is internalized.

CHAPTER FOUR

Thoughts, feelings and what you do

Hassles and problems are part of everyday life. Parents, friends, boy- or girlfriends, school, work – in fact almost everything – create problems at some time or another. Luckily, we are quite good at coping with many of these problems and they are quickly and successfully sorted out.

Other problems seem more difficult. This may be because:

▶ they happen fairly often

▶ they have been around for some time

▶ they feel totally overwhelming

▶ they seem to affect everything you do.

Sometimes these problems take over and life becomes one big unhappy worry.

The magic circle

Think Good – Feel Good aims to help you discover helpful ways of dealing with your problems. It is based on a way of helping called **cognitive behaviour therapy (CBT)**. This is an effective way of helping people to deal with their problems, and it explores the important link between:

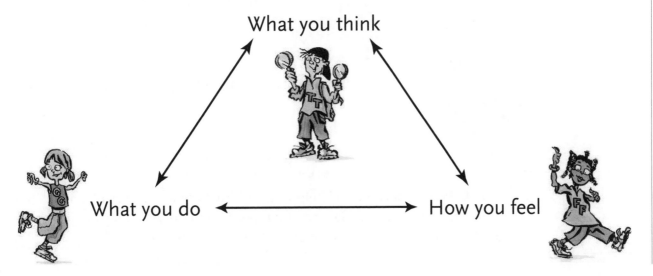

What you think

What you do ⟷ How you feel

We shall find out more about this link, although the following examples may help you understand how it works.

▶ **Thinking** that you are not very good at talking with people may make you **feel** very worried or anxious when you are out with your friends. You may **go quiet** and not talk very much.

▶ **Thinking** that no one likes you may make you **feel** sad. You may **stay at home** on your own.

▶ **Thinking** that you never get things right may make you **feel** angry. You may **give up trying** because 'it will be wrong'.

 Often, as in these examples, our thoughts magically seem to come true.

But is this really the case? Is our future so clearly set out that we are able to predict correctly what is going to happen?

Think Good – Feel Good will help you to explore this question and help you to realize that sometimes you may not see the whole picture. You may focus on only one side of the story – usually that bit which has gone wrong or isn't quite right.

Often you may not even realize what you are doing. It has become part of everyday life and it can be very difficult to see any way out or to think about how things could be different. Because of this you will probably need the help of the **Think Good – Feel Good** Team.

The **Thought Tracker** will help you look at the way you think.

The **Feeling Finder** will help you discover the way you feel.

The **Go Getter** will help you find ways to change what you do.

 Think Good – Feel Good will help you learn that the way you think and approach problems will affect what happens. Perhaps you can gain greater control over what happens in your life than you really think!

What you think

Our minds are always busy. As soon as one thought passes through, another arrives to take its place. We are constantly thinking about all sorts of things. Many of our thoughts are describing what is going on around us. Others will be about ourselves.

These might be about **the way we see ourselves**.

▶ I'm fat.

▶ I have lots of friends.

▶ I've got a bad temper.

They might be about **how we judge what we do**.

▶ I'm hopeless at organizing myself.

▶ I'm good at sports.

▶ I'm pretty good at making friends.

They might describe **our view of the future**.

▶ No one will ever want to go out with me.

▶ I'll never get to university.

▶ I'll be a millionaire by the time I'm thirty.

Core beliefs

The way we think about ourselves, judge what we do and view our future develops over time into strong patterns of thinking. These patterns of thinking are fairly fixed and become our **core beliefs**. These often appear as very short statements such as:

▶ I am kind

▶ I work hard

▶ I am successful.

Beliefs and assumptions

Core beliefs are helpful. They help us to predict and make sense of what happens in our lives. They lead us to assume that certain things will happen. This is the **'IF/THEN'** link.

▶ **IF** I am kind (core belief), **THEN** other people will like me (assumption).

▶ **IF** I work hard (core belief), **THEN** I will get a good job (assumption).

▶ **IF** I am successful (core belief), **THEN** I will be happy (assumption).

▶ Unhelpful beliefs and assumptions

Many of our core beliefs are useful, but others are less helpful. They prevent us from making real choices and decisions, and can lead us to make false assumptions about our life. Examples of unhelpful core beliefs might be:

▶ Everything I do must be perfect

▶ I always get things wrong

▶ No one will ever love me.

Core beliefs such as these often set you up to **fail**, make you **feel bad**, and **limit what you do**. They lead you to assume that negative things will happen.

▶ The **belief** that 'everything I do must be perfect' may lead you to **assume** that your work is never good enough. This may result in you feeling stressed and unhappy as each piece of work is repeated again and again.

▶ The **belief** that 'I always get things wrong' may lead you to **assume** that there is no point in working hard. You may feel sad and become unmotivated or lose interest in your work.

▶ The **belief** that 'no one will ever love me' may lead you to **assume** that people are out to make fun of you. You may feel angry and become very rude and aggressive.

▶ Core beliefs and assumptions are fairly fixed

Core beliefs and assumptions are usually very strong and become fairly fixed. They are often very resistant to any alternative challenge. Any evidence that would question them is often ignored or dismissed as unimportant.

- The girl who believes that 'no one will ever love me' may reject any signs of affection from her parents as 'they don't really care – they are just trying to get round me'.

- Anything, no matter how small, that supports these beliefs is seized upon as proof. The parent who has had a busy day and has not had time to wash that special item of clothing may be seen as evidence that 'I knew you didn't care about me'.

Important events

These core beliefs and assumptions come to the front of our thinking at certain times and are often triggered by **important events** or **experiences**.

- Being asked to complete your GCSE course work may trigger the core belief that 'everything I do must be perfect' and the assumption that 'I never get it quite right'.

- Failing your driving test may trigger the core belief that 'I always get things wrong' and the assumption that 'there is no point in trying again'.

- Being dropped by your boyfriend or girlfriend could trigger the core belief that 'no one will ever love me' and the assumption that 'people are out to hurt me'.

Automatic thoughts

Once triggered, core beliefs and assumptions produce **automatic thoughts**.

These thoughts flood into our heads and provide us with a running commentary about what is going on.

Many of these thoughts are about ourselves, and a number of them will be negative and critical.

- Being asked to complete your course work may trigger automatic thoughts like 'I don't know what to do', 'This isn't good enough' or 'I'm sure that they want more than this'.

- Failing your driving test may result in automatic thoughts like 'I really screwed this up', 'I'll never be able to drive' or 'I knew I wouldn't be able to do it'.

- A relationship ending may result in automatic thoughts like 'I knew this wouldn't last, it never does', 'He/she was just making fun of me' or 'I'll never get another boyfriend/girlfriend'.

How you feel

As we have begun to see, the way in which we think affects how we feel. Our thoughts will result in many different **feelings**.

Positive or nice thoughts often produce **pleasant feelings**.

▶ The thought 'I'm really looking forward to that party' may make you feel happy.

▶ The thought 'Although we lost I played really well' may make you feel pleased.

▶ The thought 'I look quite nice in these clothes' may make you feel relaxed.

At other times we may have more **negative** thoughts, and these often produce **unpleasant feelings**.

▶ The thought 'I bet no one will turn up to my party' may make you feel anxious.

▶ The thought 'We lost again – we will never win' may make you feel angry or sad.

▶ The thought 'I don't like these clothes' may make you feel worried and unhappy.

Many of these feelings will not be strong and will not last for very long. You may not even notice them.

At other times, these unpleasant feelings take over. They become very strong and seem to last.

The unpleasant feelings people notice most often are those of stress, unhappiness and anger.

What you do

If these feelings last or become very strong, they start to have an effect on what you do. We like to feel good, so we usually try to do more of those things that make us feel good and less of those things that make us feel unpleasant.

▶ If you feel anxious when talking with other people, you may avoid going out or turn down invitations to meet up and do things with your friends. When you stay on your own you may feel more relaxed.

▶ If you feel sad or unhappy at school, you may stop going. You may feel happier when you stay at home.

▶ If you feel angry when people criticize your work, you may give up trying so hard.

There are lots of ways in which your thoughts and feelings can affect what you do. You may notice that you:

▶ **give up** and stop doing things

▶ **avoid** situations that might be difficult

▶ become **reluctant to try** new things.

It would seem that these changes prove that our thoughts were right all along!

▶ Difficulty in concentrating would prove the thought that 'I will never pass these exams'.

▶ Staying at home would prove the thought that 'no one likes me – I haven't any friends'.

▶ Finding it difficult to sleep or putting on weight would prove the thoughts that 'I look a wreck' and 'no one would want to go out with me'.

STOP – can we look at this again?

You may be caught in a trap.

You may **ONLY** be looking for evidence to support your negative thoughts.

▶ You may have found it difficult to concentrate today – you didn't sleep very well last night. Usually you sleep better, and when you have had a good night's sleep you are able to concentrate.

▶ You may have stayed at home last night, but you have arranged to go out with your friends tomorrow.

▶ You may have gained 2 kg but does that really make such a big difference to how you look? Your favourite clothes still fit well.

Thoughts may magically come true because you are only looking for evidence that supports them. Is it possible that you are only seeing one side of the story?

We need to break out of this unhelpful cycle.

We need to learn to identify, question and test some of our negative thoughts.

Learning to develop a more balanced way of thinking will make you feel better and will enable you to make real choices about the important things in your life.

Thoughts, feelings and what you do: putting it all together

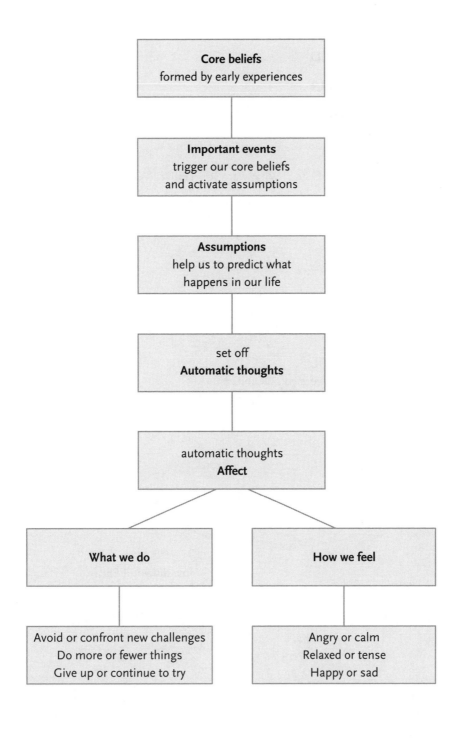

The magic circle

Think about something you have done recently which you **really enjoyed**. Write or draw in the circles below:

▶ what you **DID**

▶ how you **FELT**

▶ what you were **THINKING**.

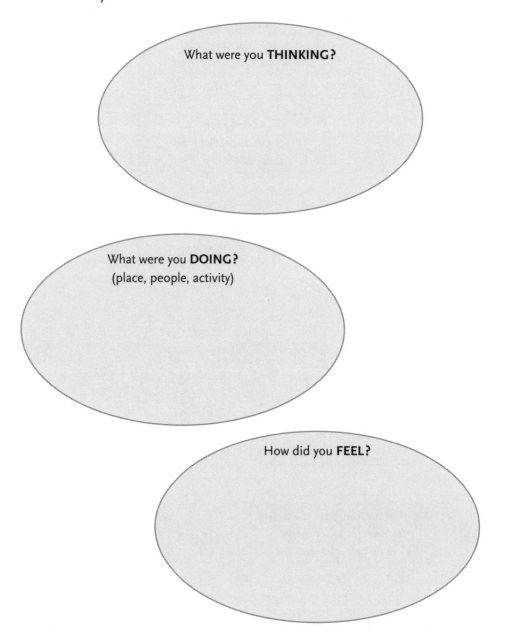

What were you **THINKING**?

What were you **DOING**?
(place, people, activity)

How did you **FEEL**?

THOUGHTS, FEELINGS AND WHAT YOU DO

The negative trap

Think about one of your **most difficult situations** and write/draw:

▶ what **HAPPENS**

▶ how you **FEEL**

▶ what you **THINK** about when you are in that situation.

What I **THINK:**

What I **DO:**

How I **FEEL:**

THOUGHTS, FEELINGS AND WHAT YOU DO

The IF/THEN quiz

Try the IF/THEN Quiz. What do you think will happen?

IF   I am good   **THEN**

IF   I get into trouble   **THEN**

IF   I get things wrong   **THEN**

IF   I work hard   **THEN**

IF   I have no friends   **THEN**

IF   People like me   **THEN**

IF   I make people happy   **THEN**

IF   I let my parents down   **THEN**

IF   I am not kind   **THEN**

IF   I am successful   **THEN**

What I think, what I do or how I feel

Are these THOUGHTS, FEELINGS or what you DO?

I am going to get this wrong

Angry

Sad

Going to school

Playing with my friends

This is really good

I'm good at making people laugh

Cross

Being on my own

People don't like me

Having a bath

Happy

Eating tea

No one will ever want to be my friend

Stressed

Frightened

I will never pass my exams

Shopping

◀ **CHAPTER FIVE** ▶

Automatic thoughts

The thoughts that quickly pop into your head throughout the day are called **automatic thoughts**. They provide you with a running commentary about what happens and what you do. We have these thoughts all the time, and they are important because they affect what we do and how we feel.

Me, what I do and my future

The automatic thoughts we are most interested in are those that are about **YOU**. They might be about any of the following.

▶ How you see yourself

▶ I'm clever.

▶ I'm not very good at getting on with people.

▶ I'm good-looking.

▶ The way you judge yourself

▶ Everything I do goes wrong.

▶ I'm hopeless at sport.

▶ I did really well in my maths test.

▶ The way you see the future

▶ One day I'll settle down.

▶ I'm never going to be happy.

▶ There are plenty of things I can do when I leave school.

These are the building blocks that form the overall picture of how you see yourself. These thoughts shape what you think about yourself, how you judge what you do, and what you expect will happen in the future.

These thoughts can be **positive**.

▶ I played well in that game.

▶ I had a really nice time with my friends tonight.

▶ Mike seems to like me.

These positive thoughts might **encourage** you to:

▶ continue training and playing sport

▶ make another arrangement to go out with your friends

▶ invite Mike round and spend more time with him.

Automatic thoughts can also be **negative**.

▶ That's the worst I've ever played.

▶ None of my friends are talking to me tonight.

▶ I'm not sure, but I don't think Mike likes me.

Negative automatic thoughts might make you **stop or avoid** doing things. You might start to:

▶ miss training sessions

▶ become less interested in going out and seeing friends

▶ avoid going to places if you know that Mike might be there.

We have a mixture of negative and positive automatic thoughts. Most people are able to see **both sides** and end up making **balanced decisions and judgements**.

Others find it harder to think about things positively. They seem to look through **negative glasses** and will only see and hear the things that are not right.

▶ Their thoughts tend to be very negative.

▶ They find it hard to think, hear or see anything good about themselves.

▶ They do not recognize any positive skills.

▶ They have a gloomy view about their future and do not believe that they could be successful.

For some people, this way of thinking takes over. Their automatic thoughts become mainly negative.

Why do I listen to my negative thoughts?

To understand this we need to learn a little more about negative automatic thoughts. They have a number of things in common.

▶ **Automatic** – they just happen. They pop up without you having to think of them.

▶ **Distorted** – when you stop and check you will find that they don't really fit all the facts.

▶ **Continuous** – you do not choose to have them and they can't easily be turned off.

▶ **Seem true** – they seem to make sense so you accept them as true without stopping to challenge and question them.

▶ Because our automatic thoughts seem very reasonable, we **listen** to them.

▶ We become **very familiar** with them because we hear them so often.

▶ The more we hear them, the more we **believe** and accept that they are true.

Our negative thoughts are like a tape being played in our head.

▶ The thoughts go round and round.

▶ The tape never gets changed.

▶ The volume is never turned down.

▶ The tape is never heard by anyone else.

The negative trap

These negative automatic thoughts become unhelpful and we end up becoming caught in a negative trap.

▶ Our negative thoughts make us feel unpleasant.

▶ Our unpleasant feelings prevent us from doing things.

▶ Doing less gives us more time to think about all the things that are going wrong.

▶ This confirms our negative thoughts.

And so it goes on and on and on.

The negative cycle

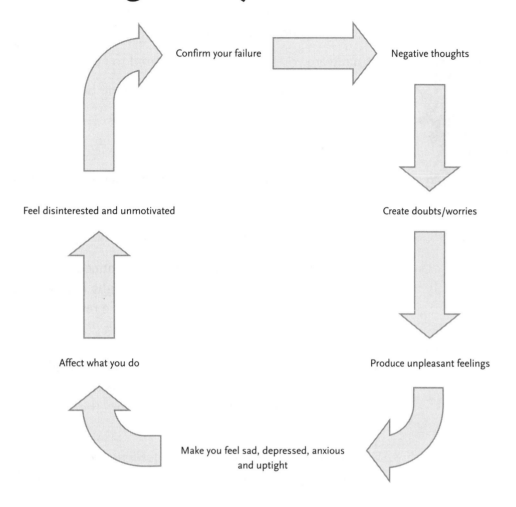

Confirm your failure → Negative thoughts

Negative thoughts → Create doubts/worries

Create doubts/worries → Produce unpleasant feelings

Produce unpleasant feelings → Make you feel sad, depressed, anxious and uptight

Make you feel sad, depressed, anxious and uptight → Affect what you do

Affect what you do → Feel disinterested and unmotivated

Feel disinterested and unmotivated → Confirm your failure

'Hot' thoughts

We have automatic thoughts all the time. However, we need to identify our **'hot'** thoughts – those that occur most often and those that are the strongest. In order to do this we need the help of the **Thought Tracker**.

As we have already seen, our automatic thoughts usually seem to be fairly reasonable. We often accept them as true without stopping to question them. In fact, we often don't even notice them. We need the **Thought Tracker** to help us to identify those thoughts that are negative and biased. The **Thought Tracker** will help us to check whether we are seeing the whole story or whether we are only focusing on one small part of what is going on.

The best place to start is to look for those thoughts that stir up the strongest feelings. These are the **'hot'** thoughts. Think about those times when you really notice a change in how you feel. Try to identify what thoughts are going through your mind when you feel like this. The following questions may help.

▶ What were you thinking **as you started** to feel this way?

▶ What were your thoughts when this feeling **became really strong?**

▶ What did you think **was going to happen?**

▶ How did you think this **would end?**

▶ What did you think **other people might say** about what happened?

▶ Sara becomes uptight

Sara was waiting at the bus stop when she noticed herself suddenly becoming very uptight and tearful. The **Thought Tracker** helped Sara to identify the **'hot'** automatic thoughts that were racing through her mind at the time.

▶ *What were you thinking as you started to feel this way?* Sara was thinking about the boy she had met at the disco last night. She liked him and was looking forward to meeting him again. Sara then started to worry that he wouldn't turn up.

▶ *What were your thoughts when your feelings became very strong?* Sara was now thinking of all the possible reasons why he might not turn up. She thought 'he didn't seem that keen on me when we left', 'he didn't ask for my telephone number', 'I bet he was just being polite – he didn't really want to meet me again'.

▶ *What did you think was going to happen?* Sara was convincing herself that the boy would not turn up.

▶ *How did you think this would end?* Sara thought that she would end up in town all on her own.

▶ *What did you think other people might say about what happened?* Sara had made a big fuss about this boy, and her friends would be keen to know what happened. She started to worry about how she would explain it, and she thought that they would all laugh at her.

This negative scene was being acted out in Sara's mind. The more she had these thoughts the worse she felt, and the more convinced she became that this would actually happen.

It is not surprising that Sara felt so uptight and sad! It all started to make sense.

- ▶ We have a constant stream of automatic thoughts running through our heads.

- ▶ Many of these thoughts are about ourselves.

- ▶ Some of these thoughts will be negative and will make us feel unpleasant.

- ▶ Identifying our negative thoughts is the first step towards learning how to feel good.

AUTOMATIC THOUGHTS

Thoughts and feelings

You need to find out more about your automatic negative thoughts and the effect that they have on you.

Fill in the diary over the next week at any time you become aware of a strong negative **'hot'** thought, or if you notice a strong unpleasant feeling. When this happens, write down the following.

▶ The date and time.

▶ Describe what was happening, who was there, and when and where it happened.

▶ What thoughts did you have? What was racing through your mind at the time? Write down exactly what you thought, and don't be embarrassed!

▶ How did this make you feel?

Don't worry about spelling or writing. As long as you can remember or read what you have written, they don't matter.

My 'hot' thoughts

Over the next week, carefully check your negative 'hot' thoughts and write down the three that you have most often about the following.

Yourself

1

2

3

What you do

1

2

3

Your future

1

2

3

Nice thoughts about myself

Fill in the thought bubbles by writing or drawing the nice thoughts that you have about yourself.

THINK GOOD – FEEL GOOD

Nice thoughts about my future

Fill in the thought bubbles by writing or drawing the nice thoughts that you have about your future.

Unpleasant thoughts about myself

Fill in the thought bubbles by writing or drawing the unpleasant thoughts that you have about yourself.

Worrying thoughts about what I do

Fill in the thought bubbles by writing or drawing the worrying thoughts that you have about the things you do.

What are they thinking?

Fill in the thought bubbles by writing or drawing what these people might be thinking.

What are they thinking?

Fill in the thought bubbles by writing or drawing what the cat and mouse might be thinking.

What are they thinking?

Fill in the thought bubbles by writing or drawing what sort of things this person might be thinking.

THINK GOOD – FEEL GOOD

What are they thinking?

Fill in the thought bubbles by writing or drawing what the cat might be thinking about the dog.

CHAPTER SIX

Thinking errors

We have begun to see that some of our 'hot' automatic thoughts are not helpful. They may make us feel unpleasant or prevent us from doing things. The problem with negative automatic thoughts is that they continue to go round and round in our heads and we seldom stop to challenge or question them. In fact, we do the opposite – the more we hear them, the more we believe them, and the more we look for evidence or select things to prove them.

These are **thinking errors**. There are six common types of thinking errors that we make.

The downers

With these types of errors we focus only on the negative things that happen. We only see the things that **go wrong or that aren't right**. Anything positive is overlooked, disbelieved or thought to be unimportant. There are two common types of downers.

 ## Negative glasses

Negative glasses only let you see one part of what happens – the negative part!

If you have a good time, or if nice things happen, the negative glasses will still find the things that went wrong or weren't quite good enough. It is these negative things that you notice and remember most.

▶ You may have had a really good day out with your friends, but at lunchtime your favourite café was full. When you are asked whether you had a good time, you reply 'No. We couldn't get into the café'.

4

▶ Positive doesn't count

With this thinking error, anything positive is dismissed as unimportant or else discredited.

▶ The person who hears that a boy or girl wants to go out with them may think 'they probably can't find anyone else to go out with'.

▶ Doing well in a maths test may be discounted as you think 'but it was easy – we learned all that last year'.

Blowing things up

The second type of thinking errors are those where negative things are blown up and **become bigger** than they really are. This happens in three main ways.

▶ All-or-nothing thinking

Everything is seen in all-or-nothing terms. It is either boiling hot or freezing cold, and there doesn't seem to be anything in between!

▶ You may have a disagreement with your best friend and think to yourself 'that's it – you're not my friend any more'.

If you fall short of perfect, then you see yourself as a total failure.

▶ Getting 72% in a maths test may cause someone to think 'I never get anything right – I'm going to give up maths'.

▶ Magnifying the negative

With this thinking error, the importance of things that happen is exaggerated. Negative events are magnified and blown up out of all proportion.

▶ 'I forgot his name and **everyone** was looking at me and laughing at me'.

▶ 'I dropped my book and the **whole class** was watching me'.

▶ Snowballing

With this thinking error, a single event or upset snowballs and quickly grows into a never-ending pattern of defeat. The first grey cloud in the sky becomes evidence of an approaching thunderstorm!

▶ Not being picked for the sports team could result in thoughts such as 'I'm no good at sports, I can't understand maths, I just **can't do anything'**.

Predicting failure

Another type of thinking error is about what we **expect** will happen. These types of errors often **predict failure** and make us expect the worse. This can happen in two main ways:

▶ The mind-reader

With this thinking error, the person thinks that they know what everyone else is thinking.

▶ 'I know she doesn't like me'.

▶ 'I bet everyone is laughing at me'.

▶ The fortune-teller

With this thinking error, the person thinks that they know what will happen.

▶ 'If we go out, I'll end up sitting on my own'.

▶ 'I know I'm not going to be able to do this work'.

Feeling thoughts

With this thinking error our **emotions become very strong** and cloud the way in which we think and see things. What we think depends on how we feel, not on what actually happens.

▶ Emotional reasoning

Because you feel bad, sad and down, then you assume that everything else is, too. Your emotions take over and colour the way in which you think.

▶ Dustbin labels

You attach a label to yourself and think of everything you do in these terms.

- ▶ 'I'm just a loser'.
- ▶ 'It's me, I'm just hopeless'.
- ▶ 'I'm rubbish'.

Setting yourself up to fail

This error is about the standards and expectations that we set ourselves. Often our **targets are too high**, and we never seem to achieve them. We set ourselves up to fail. We become very aware of our failings and the things we have not done. These thoughts often start with words such as:

- ▶ I should
- ▶ I must
- ▶ I shouldn't
- ▶ I can't.

They result in us setting impossible standards, which we can't achieve.

Blame me!

At other times **we feel responsible** for the negative things that happen, even though we have no control over them. Everything that goes wrong is down to us!

▶ 'As soon as I got on the bus, it broke down'.

▶ If your friend doesn't see you and walks past without talking to you, you may think 'I must have said something to upset him'.

It is important to remember that everyone makes these errors at some stage. The problem starts when they happen regularly and when they prevent you from making real choices about the things you can or want to do in your life.

Identifying thinking errors

Keep a diary and when you notice a negative thought, write it down. Describe what was happening and how you felt.

Use the Thought Thermometer on page 87 to rate how much you believe your negative thought.

The next day, look at your diary and fill in the last column.

▶ Were you making any thinking errors?

▶ What were they?

▶ Do you make some errors more than others?

▶ Finally, use the Thought Thermometer to rate how much you now believe your negative thought.

THINK GOOD – FEEL GOOD

Day and time	Situation What, where, when and who	Thoughts What were your thoughts Rate how much you believe them	Feelings How did you feel	Errors What thinking error are you making How much do you believe this now

What thinking errors do you make?

▶ The downers

▶ How often do you find yourself looking for the bad things that happen?

Never   **Sometimes**   **Often**   **All of the time**

▶ How often do you find yourself looking for the things that go wrong or which aren't quite good enough?

Never   **Sometimes**   **Often**   **All of the time**

▶ How often do you ignore or overlook the positive or good things that happen?

Never   **Sometimes**   **Often**   **All of the time**

▶ How often do you play down the positive or good things that happen?

Never   **Sometimes**   **Often**   **All of the time**

▶ Blowing things up

▶ How often do you find yourself using all-or-nothing thinking?

Never   **Sometimes**   **Often**   **All of the time**

▶ How often do you magnify or blow up the things that go wrong?

Never   **Sometimes**   **Often**   **All of the time**

▶ How often do single negative events seem to snowball into something bigger?

Never   **Sometimes**   **Often**   **All of the time**

THINKING ERRORS

▶ Predicting failure

▶ How often do you think you know what other people are thinking about you?

Never   Sometimes   Often   All of the time

▶ How often do you expect things to go wrong?

Never   Sometimes   Often   All of the time

▶ Feeling thoughts

▶ How often do you think that you are a stupid or bad person?

Never   Sometimes   Often   All of the time

▶ How often do you think that you are a loser who can never do anything right?

Never   Sometimes   Often   All of the time

▶ Setting yourself up to fail

▶ How often do you think that things are not good enough unless they are perfect?

Never   Sometimes   Often   All of the time

▶ How often do you find yourself thinking that you **'should'** do this or that?

Never   Sometimes   Often   All of the time

▶ How often do you find yourself saying **'I must'**?

Never   Sometimes   Often   All of the time

▶ Blame me!

▶ How often do you blame yourself for the things that happen or go wrong?

Never   Sometimes   Often   All of the time

CHAPTER SEVEN

Balanced thinking

Often we become stuck in a negative trap and find ourselves making the same thinking errors time and time again. The more we make these errors, the more we believe our negative thoughts and the harder it becomes to challenge them and see things in a different way.

In order to break out of this cycle, we have to learn to identify and challenge our negative thoughts. By doing this we shall be able to gain a more balanced view of what is going on.

Until you get used to doing it, **balanced thinking** can be hard.

It is at these times that the **Thought Tracker** can help. The **Thought Tracker** can suggest some questions that might help you to gain a more balanced view and help you to challenge your negative thoughts.

The following questions might be helpful.

 What evidence is there to **support** this thought?

 What evidence is there to **question** this thought?

 What would my **best friend**/teacher/parent say if they heard me thinking in this way?

 What would I **say to my best friend** if he or she had this thought?

 Am I making **any thinking errors**?

> ▶ Am I having a **DOWNER** on myself and forgetting my strengths (negative glasses or positive doesn't count)?

> ▶ Am I **BLOWING THINGS UP** (all-or-nothing thinking, magnifying the negative or snowballing)?

> ▶ Am I **PREDICTING FAILURE** (mind-reader or fortune-teller)?

> ▶ Are these **FEELING THOUGHTS** (emotional reasoning and dustbin labels)?

> ▶ Am I **SETTING MYSELF UP TO FAIL?**

> ▶ Am I **BLAMING MYSELF** for the things that have gone wrong?

Balanced thinking is **NOT** about rationalizing your thoughts.

Balanced thinking is **NOT** about seeing everything positively.

Balanced thinking is about looking for new information that you might otherwise overlook.

Our thoughts have to be realistic. Otherwise we would be fooling ourselves into thinking that everything is problem free – and this just isn't the case!

So how does it work?

 Sita's school work

Sita was watching television when she noticed herself becoming very tearful and feeling very stressed. The programme on TV was one of her favourites, but she hadn't really been watching it. She was thinking about other things. The **Thought Tracker** helped Sita to identify and write down the following thoughts:

❝ ◀ I've messed everything up.
◀ I'm never going to pass my examinations.
◀ Even if I started working now, it's too late.
◀ I'm just stupid. ❞

Now that Sita had identified the thoughts that were making her feel unhappy, the next stage was to check whether she was seeing the whole story. She used some of the **Thought Tracker's** questions to find out whether this really was **balanced thinking.**

▶ *What evidence is there to support these thoughts?* Sita had been struggling to complete her maths homework that evening, and no matter how she tried she just couldn't seem to do it.

- *What would her best friend Claire say?* 'You know that maths isn't your strongest subject, but you have always got through the exams. You are in the top groups for everything else'.

- *What would her maths teacher say?* 'We have only started this work today, and I think it will take all the class some time before they really understand it'.

- *What thinking errors was Sita making?*

1 *Blowing things up*
   All-or-nothing thinking – leaping from being unable to complete her maths homework to failing her examinations.
   Snowballing – failing to complete her maths homework meant that 'everything' was messed up.

2 *The downers*
   Negative glasses – not recognizing that she is in the top set for all the other subjects.

3 *Feeling thoughts*
   Dustbin labels – thinking of herself as stupid when her best friend and teachers think that she is clever.

By stopping and challenging these negative thoughts, Sita recognized that she was seeing only half of the story. Although she did not understand her maths homework, it was new work. Maths was the subject she found hardest, but so far she had always managed to pass her exams. Finally, Sita recognized that she was doing very well in her other subjects, and that there was no reason why her future should be ruined.

▶ Adam's friends

Adam was lying in bed and felt himself becoming very tense. The **Thought Tracker** helped Adam to identify the following thoughts that were racing through his head.

"◄ Mike doesn't like me anymore.
◄ He wants to be on his own.
◄ I'm too boring and serious.
◄ I annoy him'."

It was time for Adam to check whether this was **balanced thinking** or whether he was only listening to his negative thoughts. Like Sita, he used some of the **Thought Tracker's** questions to test this.

▶ *What evidence is there to support these thoughts?* Mike said he was unable to come to my house after school today. He doesn't seem very happy when we talk, and often he doesn't seem to listen to what I say.

▶ *What evidence is there to question these thoughts?* Mike slept over at my house at the weekend and he invited me to stay with him next Saturday. I know that Mike is worried about his parents at the moment and perhaps he wants to stay at home with them.

▶ *What thinking errors was Adam making?*

1　*Predicting failure*
　　The mind-reader – thinking that Mike doesn't like me.

2　*Feeling thoughts*
　　Dustbin labels – 'I'm boring' – even though we've been friends for five years.

 Adam was able to recognize that he was panicking. He and Mike were still friends and had already arranged a time to be together. Adam realized that maybe Mike was feeling unhappy and worried about something else, rather than being fed up with him.

 ▶ **Balanced thinking** is a way of testing your thoughts and checking that you are seeing the whole of the story.

▶ Look for new evidence.

▶ Think what other people would say if they could hear your thoughts.

▶ Check that you aren't making any thinking errors.

Looking for evidence

Keep a thought diary. When you find yourself having negative thoughts, **STOP** and **TEST** them.

▶ Write down your negative thoughts as clearly as you can.

▶ Use the Thought Thermometer on page 87 to rate how much you believe them.

▶ Write down the evidence that supports these negative thoughts.

▶ Write down the evidence that does not support these thoughts.

▶ What would your best friend say?

▶ What would you say to them if they had these thoughts?

▶ Use the Thought Thermometer to rate how much you believe these thoughts now.

Looking for evidence

Day and time	Thoughts What were your thoughts? Rate how much you believe them	Support What evidence supports your thoughts?	Challenge What evidence challenges this thought?	Best friend What would I say to them? What would they say to me? Rate how much you believe this now

Balanced thinking

Keep a thought diary. When you find yourself having negative thoughts, **STOP** and **TEST** them.

▶ Write down your negative thoughts as clearly as you can.

▶ Write down the evidence that supports these negative thoughts.

▶ Write down the evidence that does not support these thoughts.

The next day, look at your diary and fill in the last column (i.e. on the basis of this evidence, what would be a more balanced thought?).

Finally, use the Thought Thermometer on page 87 to rate how much you believe your balanced thought.

Balanced thinking

Day and time	Thoughts *What were your thoughts?*	Support evidence *What evidence supports your thoughts?*	Challenging evidence *What evidence does not support these thoughts?*	Balanced thought *What is a more balanced thought?* *Rate how much you believe this thought*

Thought thermometer

Use the scale to show how strongly you believe in your thoughts.

10 Very strongly believe

9

8

7 Fairly strongly believe

6

5

4 Believe a little

3

2

1 Don't really believe at all

CHAPTER EIGHT

Core beliefs

Core beliefs are the fixed statements/ideas that we have about ourselves. They help us to predict what will happen and help us to make sense of our world. These core beliefs are formed in childhood, and our early experiences develop them into fairly rigid assumptions about:

▶ how we see ourselves

▶ how we judge what we do

▶ how we view the future.

Our automatic thoughts echo our **core beliefs**. The more negative our core beliefs are, the more negative our automatic thoughts will be.

▶ Unlovable Marvin

Marvin had a core belief that no one loved him. This resulted in his having lots of automatic thoughts that proved to him that this was right.

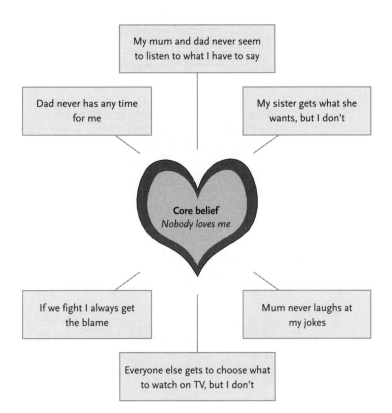

We could probably see things in a slightly different way, but Martin regarded all of these things as evidence that no one loved him.

Identifying core beliefs

The **Thought Tracker** has found a useful way to help you to identify your core beliefs.

This is called the **SO WHAT? method**.

▶ Take a negative thought and keep asking yourself **'SO WHAT? If this was true, what would this mean about me?'**

▶ Keep repeating this question until you find your core belief.

▶ **Sally is dropped from the team**

Sally felt really down after she was dropped from the netball team. She had lots of negative thoughts, so the **Thought Tracker** helped her to identify her core beliefs.

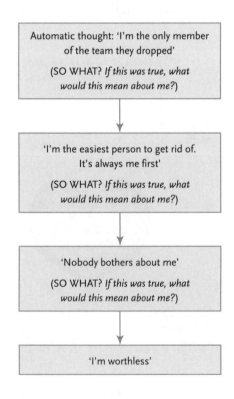

▶ James takes his exams

James received his examination marks and became very upset. Although he had obtained good marks, they didn't seem good enough to him. With the help of the **Thought Tracker**, James explored his thoughts and identified his core beliefs.

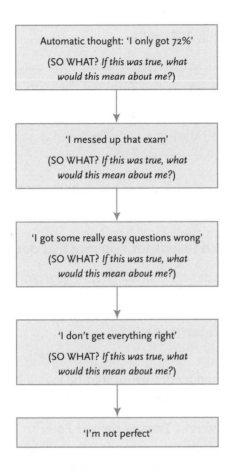

Identifying core beliefs can help you to understand why you always end up thinking the same way and how you get stuck in your negative trap.

▶ Sally has a **core belief that she is worthless**. This helped her to understand why she was always putting herself down and devaluing her achievements.

Identifying core beliefs can help you to understand why the same problems keep occurring.

▶ James has a **core belief that he must be perfect**. He tries to avoid attempting anything new or different in case he finds that he can't do it.

Challenging core beliefs

Once we have identified our core beliefs, the next step is to test them and check to see whether they really are true.

Core beliefs are like our automatic thoughts – we hear them and accept them as true without really questioning them. But we need to ask ourselves the following questions.

Are we seeing the whole of the story or are we looking through **negative glasses?**

Are we missing any evidence that would suggest that this belief is not true?

The **Thought Tracker** has found a useful way to help us to check our core beliefs.

We need to look for evidence that **does not support** our core belief.

No matter how small or unimportant it may seem, we must **FIND IT**.

 Peter is bad

Peter had a core belief that he was a bad person. He thought that he always made people unhappy, always got into trouble and was always being told off.

The **Thought Tracker** helped Peter to test this belief. For one day, Peter kept a diary of what happened in each of his lessons at school. He had to look for evidence that would question his core belief, so he wrote down whenever someone said something good or nice about him. After all, you can't be a bad person if people say good things about you!

At the end of the day, Peter's diary looked like this:

Maths   Teacher praised Peter for doing his homework
English   Nothing said
Science   Teacher made three positive comments about Peter's
          work and one comment about his positive attitude
History   Nothing said
English   Nothing said
Friends   Peter was invited back to Richard's house after
          school.

At the end of the day Peter looked at his diary. He hadn't got into trouble at all, some people had said good things about him, and Richard wanted to see him after school.

Although Peter saw these things, they were not strong enough to make him question his core belief. He dismissed what happened, saying 'It's not usually like that'.

The **Thought Tracker** helped again. Peter was making a **thinking error** – he was having a **downer**, positive doesn't count. The **Thought Tracker** suggested that Peter should keep the diary going for a week. This would check whether today had been a 'one-off' event or whether perhaps things were better than Peter realized.

Talk with someone else

Because core beliefs are very strong you may, like Peter, find that they are fairly difficult to challenge. This can lead you to reject any evidence that might suggest your core belief is not always right.

At these times it can be useful to talk with someone else. Talk with a good friend or someone close to you and find out whether they see things the same way as you. Another person may provide new information or may highlight things that you find difficult to see or believe.

> ► We are very good at looking for and finding evidence that supports our core beliefs. We do this automatically.
>
> ► Keeping a diary or a list of evidence that disagrees with your core beliefs is a useful way of checking whether they are really true.
>
> ► If you find this difficult, talk with someone else. You may be trapped and unable to remove your negative glasses. However, someone else may be able to point out the things that you are overlooking.

Identifying core beliefs

Take two of your most common automatic thoughts and use the 'SO WHAT?' technique to discover your core beliefs.

My negative thought:

▶ SO WHAT? *If this was true, what would this mean about me?*

▶ SO WHAT? *If this was true, what would this mean about me?*

Identifying core beliefs

My negative thought:

▶ SO WHAT? *If this was true, what would this mean about me?*

▶ SO WHAT? *If this was true, what would this mean about me?*

Challenging core beliefs

Select one of your core beliefs and over the next week record **any evidence**, no matter how small, that would suggest that this core belief is not always true.

CORE BELIEF:

EVIDENCE THAT DOES NOT SUPPORT IT:

Common beliefs

Use the Thought Thermometer on page 87 to rate how much you agree with each of the following statements.

It is important to be better than others at everything I do

Thought rating:

Other people are better than me

Thought rating:

No one loves or cares about me

Thought rating:

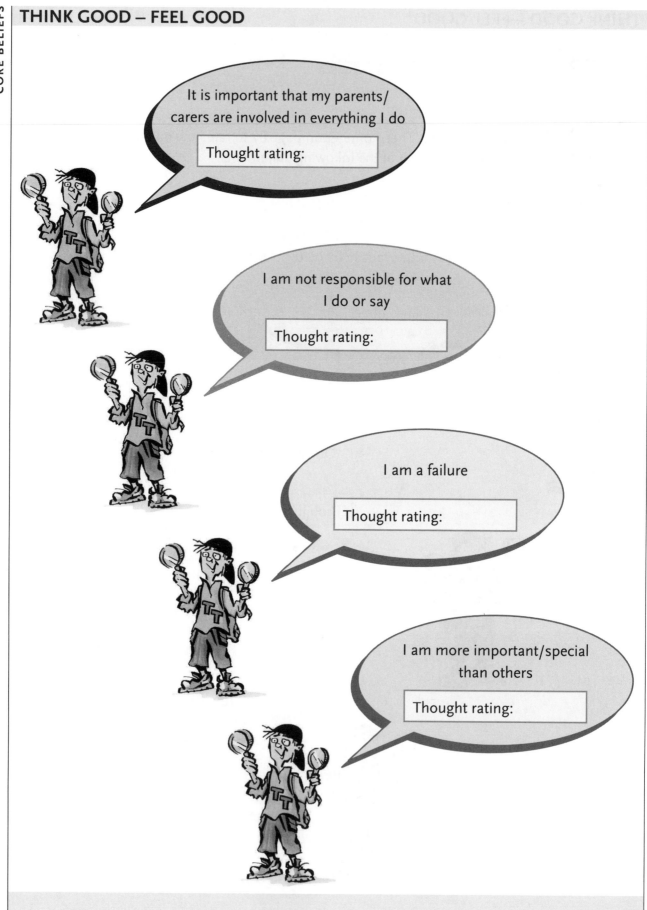

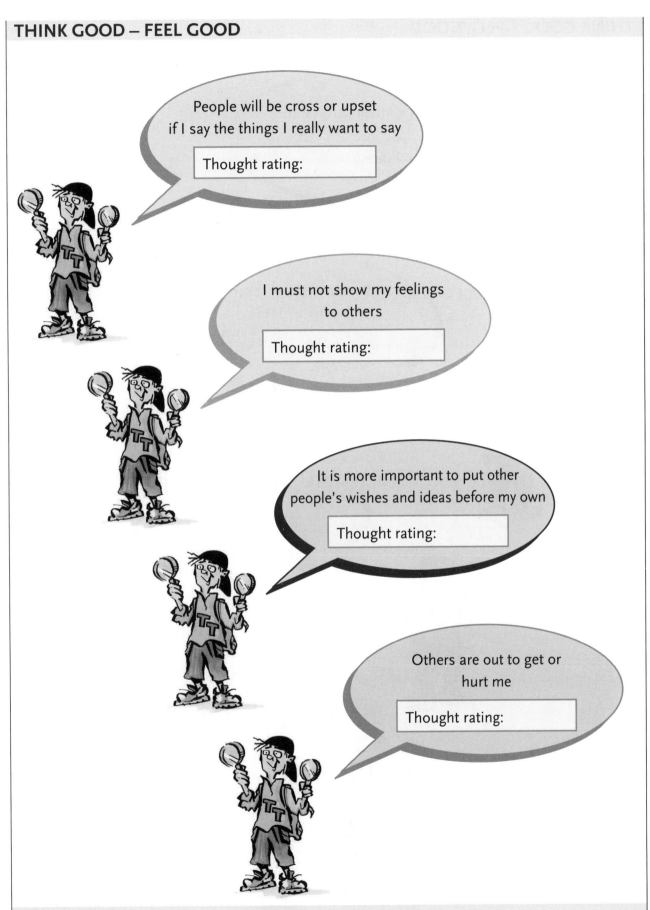

People will be cross or upset
if I say the things I really want to say

Thought rating:

I must not show my feelings
to others

Thought rating:

It is more important to put other
people's wishes and ideas before my own

Thought rating:

Others are out to get or
hurt me

Thought rating:

◀ CHAPTER NINE ▶

Controlling your thoughts

We spend a great deal of time listening to our thoughts. Some of these thoughts are negative and are about ourselves, what we do and what we expect to happen in the future. As we have already found out, we accept many of these thoughts as true without really questioning them, particularly the negative ones. We then become trapped.

▶ The negative thoughts become louder.

▶ It becomes harder to turn down the volume and hear other thoughts.

▶ The more we listen, the more unpleasant feelings we experience, and the less we end up doing.

We have started to identify some of our negative thoughts and to learn about the types of thinking errors that we make. Looking for new evidence to test these thoughts is important, and it will help us to check that our thinking is balanced.

For some people, negative thoughts and thinking errors occur so often that there just doesn't seem to be enough time in the day to check and challenge each one. Because they may occur so often, we need to find ways to stop them as soon as we notice them.

The **Thought Tracker** has some ideas to help you to regain control of your thoughts. You may not always find them easy to use, and there will probably be times when you may be aware of your thoughts but feel unable to turn them off. Try not to worry about this. If these ideas work for some of the time they are useful, but remember that the more you practise the better you will become.

Distraction

You may notice that in some situations you often feel uncomfortable or have regular negative thoughts. At these times you may want some short-term relief, and this is where **distraction** techniques may be helpful.

▶ **Distraction** helps to take your mind off your negative thoughts.

▶ **Distraction** helps you to take control of your thoughts by thinking about something else.

▶ Remember that if you continue to listen to your negative thoughts, they will become louder and take over.

The idea of **distraction** is to train yourself to keep your mind busy doing what you want it to do. You teach yourself to focus your thoughts on something else. Rather than listening to worrying or negative thoughts, you learn to drown them out by getting your mind to do what you want it to do. **Distraction** can be achieved in different ways.

▶ Describe what you see

This involves describing to yourself in detail what you see. Try to do this as quickly as you can, and think about colours, shapes, size, smells, textures, etc.

▶ Mary feels frightened

Mary often feels very frightened during her history lesson at school. She can remember a time when the teacher embarrassed her in front of her classmates. Mary still thinks about this incident and it still scares her. When Mary starts to feel frightened she worries more and often ends up thinking about how she is feeling, fearing that she will go red and pass out.

Mary needs to regain control of her thoughts. She needs to think about what is going on around her, rather than concentrating on how she is feeling. The next time she felt frightened, Mary tried describing what she saw. Her description went like this:

> ❝ I'm sitting in a class with about 15 other girls. My teacher, Mrs Evans, is standing at the front. She is wearing a black top, a red crew-neck jumper and a knee-length black skirt. There is writing on the board – today's date, Wednesday 16th, and tonight's homework, which is to copy our rough work into our books. Next to me is Sally. She is wearing a white blouse, cuffs turned back and a black skirt and tights. She has three books on her desk, all closed, and she is fiddling with her pencil. ❞

By this stage Mary was beginning to feel calmer. She had drowned out her worrying thoughts and had regained control. When she started to feel frightened again, Mary repeated this task until she felt calm and in control.

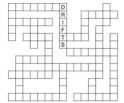

▶ Thinking puzzles

At other times you may want to occupy your thoughts by setting yourself some form of thinking puzzle. This could be anything, such as:

▶ counting backwards from 123 in nines

▶ spelling the names of your family backwards

▶ naming the records of your favourite group

▶ naming all of the players in your favourite sports team.

The puzzle has to be hard enough to challenge you, so don't make it too easy. The idea is that this task takes over and drowns out any unhelpful negative thoughts you might be having.

Absorbing activities

Some people find that they can switch off and become totally absorbed in certain activities.

Crosswords, reading, watching the television/video, playing an instrument, or listening to the radio or to music may be helpful.

The more you concentrate on what you are doing, the more you drown out any negative thoughts.

At those times when you become aware that you are listening to your negative thoughts, try one of the activities which you find helpful. For example:

▶ instead of lying in bed listening to your negative thoughts, put on your personal stereo and listen to some music

▶ Instead of worrying whether your friend will call, pick up a book and start to read it, or do a puzzle.

The more you practise the easier you will find it to block out your negative thoughts.

Coping self-talk

Negative thoughts often increase anxious or unhappy feelings. Instead of listening to your negative thoughts, try changing them by using **coping self-talk**. Coping self-talk is useful because:

▶ it can help you to feel more relaxed

▶ it can make you feel more confident

▶ it encourages you to try rather than to give up or avoid doing things.

Coping self-talk is useful if you are going to do something that really worries you. At these difficult times, instead of listening to your doubts and worries, plan to keep repeating encouraging and positive coping messages to yourself.

Positive self-talk

We are not always very good at praising ourselves for being successful. **Positive self-talk** is a way of helping us to take more notice of our achievements.

▶ Instead of thinking 'I've only answered one question – I'll never be able to finish all ten', use **positive self-talk** such as 'that's the first question finished – now for the next one'.

▶ Instead of thinking 'no one talks to me when we go out', use **positive self-talk** such as 'that was the first time Rory has ever said anything to me'.

Positive self-talk helps you to recognize that although things may not be perfect, they may be better than you think!

▶ **Amy doesn't like going out**

Amy becomes very anxious and fearful whenever she goes out of her house. She has lots of negative thoughts about what will happen, and these make her feel very anxious.

Amy decided to try coping and positive self-talk when she next went out. Instead of listening to her negative doubts and worries, she decided to think differently.

Before she went out she used her **coping self-talk**. Amy said to herself 'I'm going to do this today', 'It will be all right', 'I have been out before and everything was OK', 'I'm feeling relaxed, I'm in charge and I want to go out'.

As Amy walked down the road, she used her **positive self-talk**, with comments such as 'That's good, I'm halfway there', 'I knew I could do it', 'It's going OK' and 'I know I'm going to do it'. Amy kept repeating these thoughts to herself until she returned home.

After Amy arrived home she remembered to congratulate herself and thought 'Well done', 'That wasn't so bad after all'. She then treated herself to a long, relaxing bubble bath.

Thought stopping

Sometimes you will find that you are only able to stop your thoughts for a short time before they break through again. Another method you could use to try to control them is **thought stopping**. As soon as you become aware of the thought, follow the steps below.

▶ Immediately and loudly say **STOP**.

▶ Some people find it useful to emphasize this by banging the table or holding a chair or table tightly.

▶ Straight away think of your challenge to this negative thought and repeat it loudly to yourself.

▶ Omar goes for an interview

Omar was going for a job interview. All the time he was waiting to be interviewed negative thoughts were racing through his head:

'You're not going to get this job', 'I bet I'll go red and dry up when they ask me questions', 'I look silly in this suit'.

Omar had had enough. He was getting more and more anxious. He decided to use thought stopping. He said clearly and loudly to himself **'STOP'**.

As soon as he said this he challenged his negative thoughts and started to use his coping self-talk: 'This may not be easy, but I want this job and I'm going to try. It doesn't matter if I do go red. I'll answer their questions as well as I can'.

Omar repeated this to himself a few times and started to calm down.

With **thought stopping** you are changing the tape inside your head. Instead of listening to the constant negative tape, **thought stopping** helps you to turn it off and replace it with something more balanced.

Turn the volume down

Another way of doing this is to try to imagine the tape recorder in your head that is playing the negative tape. Imagine what the tape recorder looks like and describe it to yourself in as much detail as possible.

- ▶ What does it look like?
- ▶ What size and colour is it?
- ▶ Where are the controls?
- ▶ How do you turn it on and off?
- ▶ How do you alter the volume?

The more you concentrate on your tape, the clearer your picture will become. Once you have a good picture in your head, imagine yourself changing the settings.

- ▶ As you turn the volume up, notice how the sound becomes louder.
- ▶ As you turn the volume down, notice how the sound becomes quieter.
- ▶ As you turn the off switch, notice how silent it becomes.
- ▶ As you turn the tape on, notice how you start to hear the sound again.

Practise changing the controls. The more you practise the easier it will become. When you start to notice that you are listening to your negative thoughts, imagine the picture of your tape recorder and turn the volume down or turn the tape off altogether.

Test them

Sometimes it is useful to test your thoughts and beliefs by setting up experiments to find out whether what you expect actually happens. This is particularly useful if you often make the mind-reader and fortune-teller thinking errors, which predict that things will not work.

Julie's schoolwork

Julie did not believe that she was good at any of her school subjects. She thought that she always got her work wrong. To test this belief, Julie wrote down the results of her next 10 homework assignments.

> Core belief: I'm not clever
>
> Automatic thoughts: I always get my homework wrong. I can't do this
>
> Test: The marks I get for my next 10 homework assignments
>
> What I expect to happen (my prediction): To get poor marks (less than 6/10) for all of my homework assignments
>
> 1. English 3/10. You need to write more, Julie, and make sure that you answer the question.
>
> 2. Maths 7/10. Well done, Julie. Good work.
>
> 3. Maths 7/10. Keep it up, Julie.
>
> 4. English 4/10. Answer the questions please, Julie.
>
> 5. Geography 6/10. Nice map.
>
> 6. Art 9/10. Excellent work.
>
> 7. English 2/10. Can you please see me, Julie. This is not good enough.
>
> 8. History 5/10. Not your best work.
>
> 9. Maths 8/10. Good work.
>
> 10. English 4/10. Check your spelling and please write more neatly.

This test showed that Julie was having a problem with her English. As Julie had thought, she was getting poor marks and she wasn't answering the questions. Her history teacher also thought that she could do better, **but** the marks that Julie obtained for her other five homework assignments in maths, art and geography were good. It was possible to find a more balanced way of thinking about her schoolwork, after all.

Throw them away

Thoughts race around inside our heads.

▶ No one hears them.

▶ No one questions them.

Sometimes it is useful to empty our heads and clear our thoughts away.

At the end of the day, write down your negative thoughts on a piece of paper. If you want, you can type them on your computer and print them out.

Think of them all and write them down.

Once you have finished, scrunch up your paper tightly and throw the thoughts in the wastepaper bin!

> ▶ There are different ways in which you can take control of and challenge your thoughts.
>
> ▶ You will probably need to use a range of methods.
>
> ▶ The method that you choose will not always be successful.
>
> ▶ The more you practise the easier it will become, so stick with it.

Test your thoughts and beliefs

1 What is the negative belief/thought that you hear most often?

2 Use the Thought Thermometer on page 87 to rate how strongly you believe this thought.

3 What experiment could you set up to test whether this is true?

4 When will you carry out your test?

5 If your belief/thought was true, what do you predict would happen?

6 What did happen?

7 Use the Thought Thermometer to rate how strongly you now believe this thought.

The thought challenger

With the help of the Thought Tracker, identify the unhelpful or negative thoughts that you hear most often.

My most common negative thought is . . .

Look at **all** the evidence. What would be a more balanced thought?

A more balanced thought is . . .

Whenever you notice this negative thought:

1 say **STOP** to yourself

2 repeat your balanced thought two or three times – this will help to turn down the volume of the negative thought.

▶ It is useful to practise balanced thinking. As you get up each morning, repeat your balanced thought to yourself two or three times.

▶ Don't just listen to your negative thoughts. Challenge them and turn down the volume.

Looking for the positive

We always seem to notice the things that aren't quite right, but we are not very good at noticing the positive or good things that happen.

Each night before you go to bed, think of three things that have happened that have made you feel good. These could be anything, such as:

- nice thoughts about yourself
- positive thoughts about what you have done or achieved
- activities that have made you feel good
- things that others have said which made you feel good.

Each day write down three things, either in a private diary or on a large sheet of paper on your bedroom wall.

If you can't think of three good things, then ask someone to help you.

- Watching the list grow will help you to realize that positive things do happen to you.

Positive self-talk

We are not very good at recognizing our achievements. Often we think about the things that have gone wrong or which aren't quite right. When this happens it is useful to challenge our negative thoughts with positive self-talk.

Write down some of your negative thoughts at the end of each day.

My negative thoughts were:

Check your thoughts and see if you have missed anything positive.

The positive things I missed were:

What would be your positive self-talk?

> ► You may find this difficult at first, but don't worry. The more you practise the easier it will become.
>
> ► The next time you hear your negative thoughts, turn them off, look for success and use positive self-talk.

Coping self-talk

Some of our thoughts are not helpful. In fact, they make us feel more anxious or worried. These thoughts make us think that things will go wrong and make us expect that bad things will happen. Learning to identify and replace these thoughts with coping self-talk will help you to feel better.

With the help of the Thought Tracker, think about a situation or event that makes you feel anxious or unpleasant. When you are in this situation, write down or draw a picture of the thoughts that race through your mind. Once you have done this, think about how you can challenge these thoughts with coping self-talk.

 The situation or event that makes me feel anxious or worried is:

 The thoughts that make me feel anxious are:

 My coping self-talk is:

 The next time you are in that situation, use coping self-talk to help you to feel better.

The 'worry safe'

Sometimes it is difficult to stop worrying and turn off the thoughts that are going around in our heads.

When this happens, it may be useful to draw these thoughts or write them down on paper and lock them away!

▶ Find a box and make your own worry safe. Paint and colour it as you like and choose a place to keep it.

▶ When you find that you can't stop your worries, find some paper and draw them or write them down.

▶ Once you have finished, lock them away in your safe.

▶ At the end of the week, unlock your safe and talk about your worries with Mum, Dad or someone you trust.

▶ Once your worries are in the safe they will find it harder to trouble you.

Turn the tape off

Sometimes you may hear the same worries or negative thoughts over and over again. It is like listening to a tape that is being played inside your head.

▶ The tape goes round and round.

▶ The same thoughts are heard over and over again.

▶ The tape never gets changed.

▶ The volume is never turned down.

At these times it is useful to learn how to turn the tape off.

Step 1: Imagine your tape player

■ Imagine a picture of a tape player going round and round inside your head.

■ You may find that looking at a real tape player can help you to get a good picture.

■ Really look at the tape player and see how you can turn it on and off, where you put the tape, and how you can change the volume.

Step 2: Imagine stopping the tape

■ Think of this picture and imagine yourself putting a tape in the player.

■ As you switch it on, the tape starts and you hear your worries and negative thoughts.

■ Now imagine turning the tape player off. Really concentrate on the 'off' switch, and as you touch the button notice how the thoughts stop.

■ Practise turning the tape player on and off, and notice how the 'off' button stops your negative thoughts.

Remember that the more you practise the easier it will become.

Practise being successful

When faced with new or difficult challenges, we often think that we shall not be successful. We are very good at predicting failure and thinking that things will go wrong.

Thinking like this will make us feel anxious and reluctant to try anything new or challenging.

A useful way forward is to imagine a picture of your challenge and to talk yourself through what will happen, but this time change the ending so that you are successful.

Step 1: Imagine your challenge

Make your picture as real as possible and describe your challenge in plenty of detail. Think about:

- who will be there
- the time of day
- what you are wearing
- the colours, smells and sounds.

Step 2: Talk yourself through your challenge

Now think about what will happen. Talk yourself through your challenge.

- What will you do?
- What will you say?
- What will the other people do?
- What will they say?
- What will happen?

Practising a few times will help you to prepare yourself, and may help you to recognize that although it might be difficult, you can start to imagine what it is like to be successful.

Thought stopping

Sometimes the same unhelpful thoughts go round and round in our heads. The more we hear them:

▶ the more we believe them

▶ the more we look for evidence that supports them.

When we check them out we often find that we are only seeing part of the picture – usually the negative part. It is important to try to stop these thoughts.

A useful way of doing this is to wear an elastic band on your wrist.

When you notice that you are listening to the same unhelpful thoughts, snap the elastic band.

The elastic band will hurt a little, but this will probably stop these thoughts!

How you feel

Each day you will probably notice yourself having a range of different feelings. For example, you could:

▶ wake up feeling **anxious** about going to school

▶ feel **happy** on the school bus talking with friends

▶ feel **angry** when your friend forgets to bring the CD you wanted to borrow

▶ feel **stressed** about completing your history homework

▶ feel **relaxed** when watching TV at the end of the day.

You will find that:

▶ some of these feelings will last only a **short time**

▶ others will go **on and on**

▶ some will be so **weak** that you may not even notice them

▶ others will be **very strong** and seem to take over.

Our first job is to find out more about the types of feelings that you have. This is not always easy because:

▶ we are not always very good at identifying our feelings

▶ we often wrap all our feelings up together under one label.

To help you to discover your feelings, you may need the help of the **Feeling Finder**. The **Feeling Finder** can help you to discover:

▶ what feelings you have

▶ what feelings are the strongest

▶ where you are most likely to have these feelings

▶ what thoughts go with these feelings.

What feelings do I have?

Learning to identify your feelings is important, as it may help you to learn how to control them. For example, breathing exercises may help with feelings of anxiety or worry, but not with feelings of sadness.

Three of the strongest and most common unpleasant feelings are stress, unhappiness and anger.

▶ Stress

When people feel stressed or wound up they notice a number of different symptoms. The signs of stress vary from one person to another but may include:

- ▶ feeling sick
- ▶ butterflies in the stomach
- ▶ shortness of breath
- ▶ sweating
- ▶ legs feeling heavy or like jelly
- ▶ going red in the face
- ▶ feeling light-headed
- ▶ fainting
- ▶ aching muscles
- ▶ your mind going blank
- ▶ difficulty in making decisions.

▶ Unhappiness

Everyone feels unhappy at some time or another, but for some people this feeling takes over their life and they end up feeling very depressed. They might find themselves:

- ▶ regularly tearful
- ▶ crying for no clear reason or over small things

- ▶ waking up early in the morning
- ▶ having difficulty in falling asleep at night
- ▶ feeling constantly tired and lacking in energy
- ▶ comfort eating or losing their appetite
- ▶ having difficulty in concentrating
- ▶ losing interest in things that they used to enjoy
- ▶ going out less often.

Because these feelings produce some very strong physical reactions, people sometimes end up thinking that they are ill or unwell. These symptoms then become the reason why they stop or avoid doing things.

- ▶ 'I'm not sleeping and can't concentrate, so I have given up my weekend job'.

These physical reactions are very real, but you may not be unwell. It may be part of a trap where your negative thoughts create these symptoms. If you are unsure or want some reassurance, then check this by talking with your doctor.

▶ Anger

Anger is a very common feeling and can be expressed in many different ways:

- ▶ shouting, yelling and screaming
- ▶ swearing and threatening
- ▶ throwing things
- ▶ breaking things
- ▶ slamming doors
- ▶ hitting, kicking, fighting
- ▶ wanting to harm oneself.

Feelings and what you do

Feelings don't just suddenly happen. There is usually something that triggers them. If you remember the **Magic Circle**, then you will remember that how you feel will be affected by what you do and what you think.

The **Feeling Finder** has helped people to learn that they have different feelings in **different places**.

- ▶ At school you may feel **anxious**.
- ▶ At home you may feel **relaxed**.
- ▶ In town you may feel **worried**.

You will notice different feelings when you engage in **different activities**.

- ▶ When watching TV you may feel **calm**.
- ▶ When talking with people you may feel **anxious**.
- ▶ When doing maths you may feel **happy**.
- ▶ When playing sport you may feel **tense**.

You will also notice that you feel different with **different people**.

- ▶ With your dad you may feel **angry**.
- ▶ With your best friend you may feel **relaxed** and confident.
- ▶ With your teacher you may feel **happy**.
- ▶ With your sister you may feel **stressed**.

Feelings and what you think

The way in which we think causes feelings.

- ▶ If you **think** that you have no friends, you may **feel sad**.
- ▶ If you **think** that you are disliked, you may **feel worried**.
- ▶ If you **think** that you did well with your homework, you may **feel pleased**.

Putting it all together

If you put all this together, you will probably start to notice a pattern.

What you do	How you feel	What you think
Stay at home alone	Sad	I've got no friends
Go out with Jim	Happy	We always have a laugh together
Go to school	Stressed	I just can't keep up with my work
Go shopping for clothes	Angry	I can never find anything that looks good on me
Have a bath	Relaxed, calm	It's nice lying here

▶ How we feel depends on what we do and what we think.

▶ Try to identify the different feelings that you have.

▶ Check whether your strongest feelings are linked to particular thoughts or what you do.

Thoughts and feelings

Thoughts that make me feel **GOOD**:

1

2

3

Thoughts that make me feel **UNPLEASANT**:

1

2

3

Activities and feelings

Activities or things that make me feel **GOOD**:

1

2

3

Activities or things that make me feel **UNPLEASANT**:

1

2

3

HOW YOU FEEL

The Feeling Finder word search

Can you find these feelings that the **Feeling Finder** has hidden?

Happy	Angry	Afraid	Scared
Grumpy	Tense	Anxious	Unhappy
Worried	Wound up	Sad	Uptight
Depressed	Calm	Tearful	Excited
Relaxed	Guilty	Ashamed	Insecure
Frightened	Nervous	Hurt	Confused
Upset	Mad		

N	H	C	K	H	G	F	D	S	E	W	T	Y	U	N	F	C
H	A	N	G	R	Y	M	M	L	Q	U	P	T	I	G	H	T
C	P	W	R	K	F	B	D	I	A	N	G	F	F	X	Z	E
O	P	G	U	I	L	T	Y	N	P	H	M	N	N	G	F	A
N	Y	T	M	T	F	X	Z	S	C	A	R	E	D	S	W	R
F	E	Y	P	V	T	Y	D	E	S	P	I	R	Q	E	R	F
U	F	H	Y	N	E	L	P	C	T	P	R	V	G	J	K	U
S	D	F	G	H	N	P	R	U	G	Y	F	O	V	B	N	L
E	A	J	H	J	S	A	D	R	H	I	R	U	G	H	F	W
D	N	N	U	K	E	Y	E	E	J	K	G	S	M	K	R	D
F	X	B	R	A	D	Y	P	S	K	C	F	F	A	J	I	F
W	I	V	T	F	R	H	R	E	L	A	X	E	D	H	G	G
H	O	C	B	R	F	H	E	D	X	L	W	Q	U	L	H	H
J	U	U	B	A	V	A	S	H	A	M	E	D	P	O	T	Y
K	S	P	N	I	V	B	S	H	S	Z	S	X	T	Y	E	T
M	D	S	W	D	N	V	E	X	C	I	T	E	D	M	N	R
N	F	E	P	V	U	L	D	K	J	L	A	Z	P	L	E	Y
R	G	T	D	C	Q	P	O	W	O	R	R	I	E	D	D	J

Which are the most common feelings that you have?

THINK GOOD – FEEL GOOD

What feeling goes where?

We have different feelings in different places. Use a different colour and draw a line from each place to the feeling that best describes how you feel.

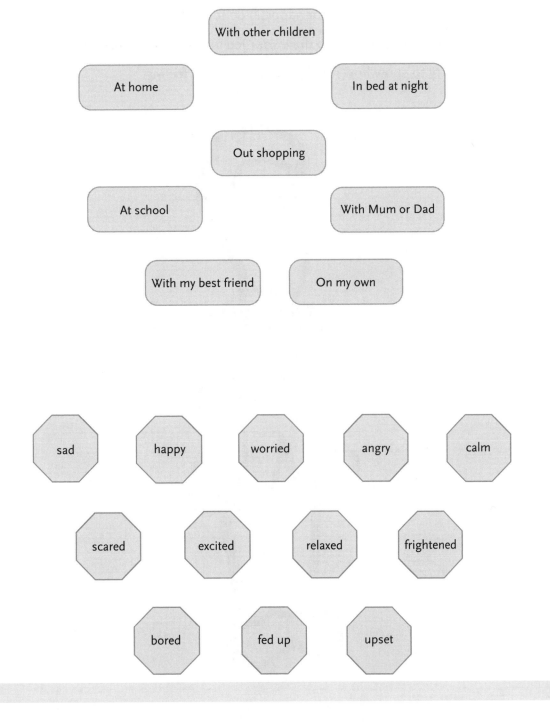

With other children

At home

In bed at night

Out shopping

At school

With Mum or Dad

With my best friend

On my own

sad   happy   worried   angry   calm

scared   excited   relaxed   frightened

bored   fed up   upset

My feelings

▶ Think about all the different feelings you have (pleasant and unpleasant) and draw or write them down on a piece of paper.

▶ Choose a coloured pen or pencil for each feeling (you could choose something like red for happy, blue for sad, etc.).

▶ Use these colours to draw your feelings on the picture below.

▶ Try to show how much you have of each feeling.

What happens when I feel sad?

Think about something that made you feel really sad and unhappy. How would someone else know that you felt like this?

What does your face look like when you are sad?

How does your body show that you are unhappy?

How do you behave when you are unhappy?

How much of the time do you feel unhappy?

Never								All the time	
1	2	3	4	5	6	7	8	9	10

What happens when I feel angry?

Think about something that made you feel really cross and angry. How would someone else know that you felt like this?

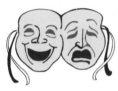

What does your face look like when you are angry?

How does your body show that you are angry?

How do you behave when you are angry?

How much of the time do you feel angry?

Never   All the time
 1   2   3   4   5   6   7   8   9   10

What happens when I feel anxious?

Think about something that made you feel really anxious or uptight. How would someone else know that you felt like this?

What does your face look like when you are anxious or uptight?

How does your body show that you are anxious or uptight?

How do you behave when you are anxious or uptight?

How much of the time do you feel anxious or uptight?

Never   All the time
   1   2   3   4   5   6   7   8   9   10

What happens when I feel happy?

Think about something that made you feel really happy. How would someone else know that you felt like this?

What does your face look like when you are happy?

How does your body show that you are happy?

How do you behave when you are happy?

How much of the time do you feel happy?

Never   All the time

1   2   3   4   5   6   7   8   9   10

Feelings and places

Think about all your different feelings and write them on sheets of paper.

Make a list of the main places, people and activities in your life. The list might include some of the following:

1 Mum

2 Dad

3 grandparents

4 best friend

5 other children

6 school

7 home

8 leisure/activity club

9 playing sport, games, reading a book

10 in bed at night

11 watching TV

12 doing schoolwork

13 going somewhere new

14 going to school

15 being with friends.

Choose which feelings go with each of the above.

What gives you the most pleasant feelings?

What gives you the most unpleasant feelings?

The Feeling Thermometer

Use the Feeling Thermometer to show how strong your feeling is.

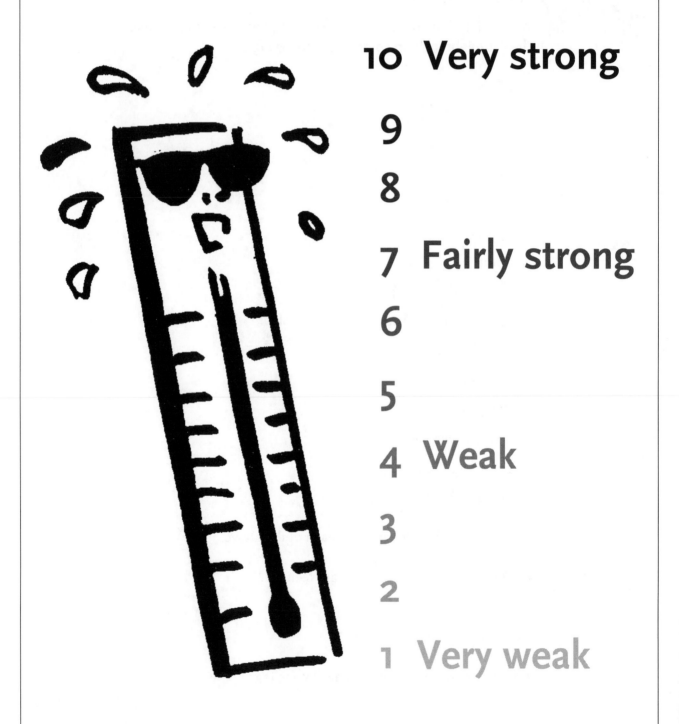

10 **Very strong**

9

8

7 **Fairly strong**

6

5

4 **Weak**

3

2

1 **Very weak**

◀ CHAPTER ELEVEN ▶

Controlling your feelings

The **Feeling Finder** has helped us to discover that the places we go to or the things we do may sometimes produce strong feelings. For example, you may notice that you:

▶ feel **anxious** when you **go out**

▶ feel **calm** and safe at **home**

▶ feel **worried** when you are **with others**

▶ feel **relaxed** and happy **on your own**.

We try to do things or go to places that give us pleasant feelings, and we try to avoid those that make us feel unpleasant.

This seems to make sense. After all, none of us want to feel unpleasant for most of the day.

But sometimes your feelings take over and **stop or limit** what you really want to do.

▶ You may **want** to go out, but because you feel so anxious you **feel unable** to go.

▶ You may **want** to be with friends, but because you feel so worried you **feel unable** to see them.

▶ You may **want** to call up a friend, but because you feel so unhappy you **feel unable** to do this.

At these times, the way you feel is stopping or preventing you from doing those things that you really want to do. Learning how to control your feelings will help to break down these barriers.

The **Feeling Finder** has found that we can learn to control our feelings in different ways.

Learn to relax

There are different ways in which you can learn to relax. Some methods will take you through a series of physical exercises to tense and then relax each of the large muscle groups in your body. Others will teach you to imagine relaxing pictures in your mind, and these calming images will help you to feel more pleasant. It is important to remember the following points.

▶ There is no **one way** of relaxing.

▶ People find **different methods** useful at different times.

▶ It is important to **find what works for you**.

▶ Physical relaxation

This method usually takes about 10 minutes and is very useful if you feel constantly tense or wound up. Using a series of short exercises, all of the major muscle groups in your body are tensed for about 5 seconds and then relaxed.

Concentrate on what the muscles feel like when they are tensed and what they feel like when they are relaxed. You will find that some parts of your body will be more tense than others, so try to find the very tense areas.

By the end of the session you should feel completely relaxed, so enjoy this pleasant feeling. A number of people like to do these exercises before they go to bed. It does not matter if you fall asleep. Like everything else, the more you practise the better and faster you will become at relaxing.

There are various tapes which you can buy that will teach you how to relax. Choose one you like and find restful. If you can't find one, then try the following exercises. Before you start, remember the following points.

▶ Choose somewhere warm and quiet.

▶ Sit in a comfortable chair or lie on your bed.

▶ Choose a time when you will not be interrupted.

▶ Tense your muscles just enough to notice what it feels like. Don't overdo it.

▶ Tense your muscles for about 3–5 seconds.

▶ Tense each muscle group twice.

▶ After you have tensed a muscle, try not to move it again.

▶ Quick relaxation exercises

Arms and hands: Clench your fists and push your arms straight out in front of you.

Legs and feet: Push your toes downwards, gently raise your legs, and stretch them out in front of you.

Stomach: Push out your tummy muscles, take a breath and hold it.

Shoulders: Scrunch up your shoulders.

Neck: Push your head back against the chair or bed.

Face: Screw up your face, squeeze your eyes tight and push your lips together.

Physical exercise

Some people find that **physical exercise** is as effective as systematically tensing and relaxing their muscles. After all, physical exercise does exactly the same thing – it tenses and then relaxes your muscles.

A good run, quick walk or swim can help you to get rid of any angry or anxious feelings.

If physical exercise works for you, then use it. It may be particularly useful to try it at those times when you notice strong unpleasant feelings.

Controlled breathing

There are times when you may suddenly start to become tense or angry, and on these occasions you won't have time to go through the relaxation exercises.

Controlled breathing is a quick method in which you concentrate and gain control of your breathing. You can use this method anywhere, and often people don't even notice what you are doing!

Slowly draw in a deep breath, hold it for 5 seconds and then very slowly let it out. As you breathe, say to yourself 'relax'. Doing this a few times will help you to regain control of your body and help you to feel calmer.

Calming pictures

With this method you make yourself feel more pleasant by thinking about the things that you find pleasant or restful.

Think about your dream place. It could be somewhere you have been or an imaginary place. Imagine a picture of it and make the picture as restful and peaceful as possible. Try to make the picture as real as you can, and think about the following:

▶ the noise of the waves crashing on the beach

▶ the wind blowing in the trees

▶ the smell of the sea or the scent of pine forests

▶ the warm sun shining on your face

▶ the wind blowing gently in your hair.

Practise imagining your relaxing place, and if you start to feel unpleasant, then try turning the picture on. Really concentrate hard on your restful scene and see if it helps you to relax.

Relaxing activities

There will probably be some things that you enjoy doing and which make you feel good. Examples of these might include:

▶ reading a book

▶ watching TV

▶ listening to music

▶ taking the dog for a walk.

If a particular activity makes you feel good, then try doing it when you notice unpleasant feelings. You may only be able to do this at certain times, but if you are:

▶ sitting around on your own worrying about tomorrow, try reading a book

▶ sitting in your bedroom feeling unhappy, try watching TV

▶ lying in bed feeling uptight because you can't sleep, try listening to some music

▶ feeling uptight, then take the dog for a walk.

Experiment and see if you can stop your unpleasant feelings.

Prevention

Sometimes we are aware of our feelings, but often we leave it too late to do something about them. At these times our feelings become too strong and no matter what we do we just can't seem to regain control. We need to learn to identify these times so that we can try to control our feelings **BEFORE** they get too strong.

▶ Jimmy's temper

Jimmy often felt very angry and became very wound up. This seemed to happen very quickly, and when he lost his temper it took him a long time to calm down afterwards.

He travelled up the anger escalator very quickly, and before he could stop, Jimmy had exploded. The **Feeling Finder** tried to help Jimmy to gain more control over his angry feelings. The **Feeling Finder** suggested that they should draw an anger volcano to help Jimmy to discover what happens as he becomes angry.

Hit them

Swear, red face, mind blank

Clench fists, grit teeth, angry face, threaten

Seems like a dream
Watching myself from above

Thoughts: 'Stop it', 'I'm going to hit you'
Feels hot and starts to sweat

Thoughts: 'You're trying to wind me up'
Normal voice and volume, feels calm

Once Jimmy became aware of his anger build-up, the next stage was to learn how **to bail out** at an early stage and prevent himself from exploding.

Jimmy was able to do this by imagining the last time he lost his temper. He imagined the picture as clearly as he could, but this time he changed the ending.

▶ Jimmy imagined himself **bailing out** before he lost his temper.

▶ He imagined himself walking away.

▶ He imagined the look of disappointment on the faces of the others who were teasing him.

▶ He imagined how pleased with himself he felt.

▶ He practised listening to the taunts of the other children and staying calm.

Jimmy practised every day. He was practising a different ending, so he was better prepared and this helped him to cope with the teasing the next time it happened.

There are many different things you can do to help you to feel better.

► Choose those methods that feel right for you.

► Remember that they won't always work, but do stick with them.

► The more you practise the more likely it is that these methods will help.

The 'feeling strong room'

We all have unpleasant feelings, but sometimes these feelings become very strong and are difficult to get rid of. They could make you feel:

▶ very angry

▶ very sad

▶ very frightened.

When you feel very unpleasant you may want to try locking these feelings away somewhere safe so that they do not bother you so much.

▶ Find a box, make it into your **'strong room'** and decorate it as you wish.

▶ When you feel very unpleasant, get some paper and write or draw your feelings.

▶ Think about what is making you feel like this and write about or draw a picture of this, too.

▶ Once you have finished, put these feelings away in the 'strong room'.

▶ At the end of the week, open your box and talk about your feelings with Mum, Dad or someone you trust.

▶ Putting your unpleasant feelings away in a strong room may help you to feel better.

CONTROLLING YOUR FEELINGS

Anger volcano

Think about how your body feels when you are calm and how it feels when you are angry. Plot the changes you notice as you become angrier on to your Anger Volcano.

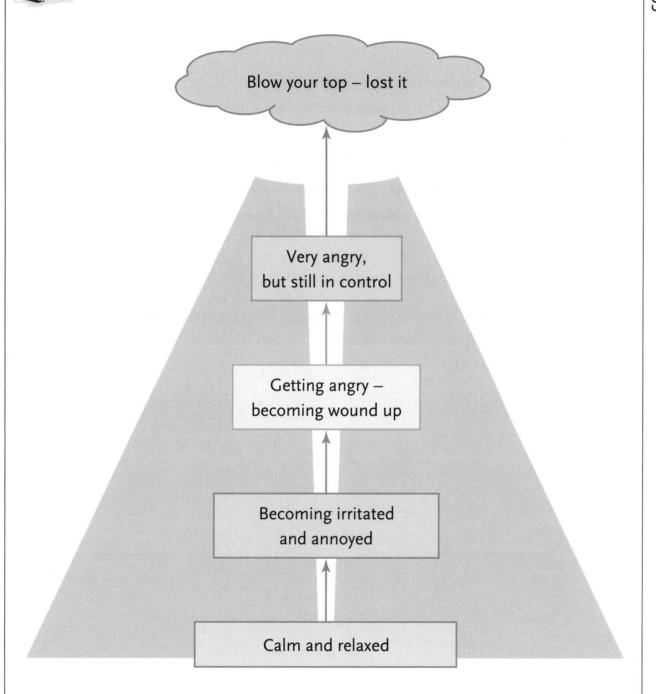

Blow your top – lost it

Very angry, but still in control

Getting angry – becoming wound up

Becoming irritated and annoyed

Calm and relaxed

Learning to relax

For younger children, learning to relax can be made fun.

Muscles can be stretched and tensed by playing a game such as 'Simon Says', in which the child is asked to do the following.

1 March straight and upright around the room.

2 Run on the spot.

3 Pretend that their arms are branches of a tree by waving them above their head.

4 Screw up their face to look like a scary monster.

5 Stretch up to the sky and be as tall as possible.

6 Roll up tightly to become as small as possible.

After the child has stretched their muscles, the final stage is to tell them to calm down and relax. Ask them to pretend to be a big heavy animal and to move around the room very slowly. Move as quietly and as slowly as possible. Finally, ask them to be 'sleeping lions' and to lie on the floor as still and quiet as possible for a couple of minutes.

My relaxing place

A useful way of relaxing is to try to imagine a calming picture.

This could be a real place you have been to or a picture you may have created in your dreams.

▶ Choose a quiet time when you will not be disturbed.

▶ Shut your eyes and imagine your picture.

▶ Really concentrate on your calming scene and imagine it in lots of detail.

▶ Think about the colours and shapes of things.

▶ Imagine the sounds – seagulls calling, leaves rustling, waves crashing on the sand.

▶ Think about the smell – the smell of pine from the trees, the smell of the sea.

▶ Imagine the sun warming your back or the moonlight shining through the trees.

▶ As you think of your picture, notice how calm and relaxed you have become.

▶ This is your special calming place.

You will need to try to practise this. The more you practise the easier you will find it to imagine your picture and the quicker you will become calm.

Whenever you feel yourself becoming stressed, think of your calming picture.

My relaxing activities

Fill in the thought bubbles by writing or drawing the things that help you to relax and feel calm.

CHAPTER TWELVE

Changing your behaviour

The **Thought Tracker** has helped us to discover that sometimes we have negative and unhelpful thoughts. We think that things will be difficult. We expect and predict the worse. Sometimes it is hard to see anything positive. The **Feeling Finder** has helped us to understand that these thoughts may make us feel uncomfortable. We may try to make ourselves feel better by:

▶ **avoiding** situations that we think will be difficult

▶ **withdrawing** and staying where we feel safe

▶ **stopping** doing things that might make us feel unpleasant.

This may bring some immediate relief, but over time you will probably feel worse. As you do less you may find yourself feeling more and more down. Anything new needs an even greater effort, and it becomes harder to tackle any new challenges. Strong unpleasant feelings flood back as you feel cross and disappointed with yourself.

And so it goes on . . .

and on . . .

and on . . .

An important way of breaking out of this trap is to become more active and take control.

Push yourself to do things.

As you become busier you will notice a number of benefits.

 You feel better

Becoming more active means that you have less time to notice any unpleasant feelings or to listen to any negative thoughts. You will start to feel better.

You feel more in control

You start to regain control of your life and do the things that you want to do.

 You feel less tired

Doing nothing is very tiring! You will feel very lethargic and exhausted. Although it sounds silly, the more active you become, the less tired you feel.

 You want to do more

The hardest thing is to get started. Once you become active you will want to do more. Quite simply, the more you do, the more you feel like doing.

 Your thinking becomes clearer

Doing nothing makes you feel sluggish both mentally and physically. Activity sharpens up your thinking.

Increase fun activities

The first and hardest job is to get going again. A useful way to do this is to increase your enjoyable activities. Set yourself targets to increase the number of enjoyable activities that you do each day or week.

Make a list of the things you enjoy/want to do and those activities that you used to enjoy and have now stopped.

These can be any activities at all, and remember that they don't have to cost money. They could be:

▶ *social activities* – talking to a friend, having someone round for tea

▶ *outdoor activities* – going for a walk, swimming, shopping

▶ *indoor activities* – listening to music, watching a video, reading a book, drawing.

From your list, choose the activity that you would most like to do. Choose a day, set a time and do it! Gradually build more and more enjoyable activities into your life.

> ▶ Don't expect the activities to be as much fun as they used to be. It will take time for your sense of enjoyment to return.
>
> ▶ Think about what you have achieved, not the other things you still have to do.
>
> ▶ **Take time to tell yourself how well you have done! After all, you deserve it.**

Map how you feel and what you do

There will probably be certain times of the day/week when you are more likely to notice strong pleasant or unpleasant feelings. It may be useful to tune into these and find out whether there are any patterns or particularly difficult times.

A useful way of doing this is to keep a diary.

▶ Write down what you are doing and how you feel each hour. Use the Feeling Thermometer on page 134 to rate how strong your feelings are.

▶ At the end of the week, look at the diary and see if there are any particularly bad/good times and whether any activity made you feel better/worse.

If you find a link between certain activities and strong feelings, then try planning your time differently. Where possible, try to do more of those activities that make you feel good and less of those that make you feel bad.

▶ Jane gets ready for school

Jane got up at 6.30 a.m. each day to go to school. She was dressed and ready to go by 7.15 and then sat around for the next 45 minutes. During this time she would worry about school, her work and what she would say to her friends. By 8.00, when it was time to leave home, she felt very worried and unhappy and often felt unable to go to school.

Once Jane had identified this pattern, she tried to arrange her morning routine differently. She got up later, at 7.30. This meant that all her time before leaving for school was now taken up. She was busy and had less time to worry about what might happen.

At other times when she woke up early she got herself ready for school, but instead of sitting in a chair, she practised her musical instrument until it was time to leave the house. Jane found that her music helped her to feel relaxed. She was busy, she felt calm, and her mind was no longer playing tricks on her.

▶ Mary returns home

Mary was always the first home from school and had one hour on her own before anyone else arrived. She kept a diary and discovered that this was the worst time of the day for her. She felt very scared of being on her own and thought that horrible things would happen to her.

Mary decided to change her routine. Instead of coming straight home after school, she planned something different. She arranged to do the things she enjoyed. She went shopping, visited friends and went to the library. She now arrived home at the same time as the rest of her family feeling calmer and happier.

Small steps

Sometimes starting an activity might seem too large a step to tackle all in one go.

▶ At these times it might be useful to break down the task into smaller steps.

▶ Each smaller step feels more manageable.

▶ This increases the chances of success, and each step will move you closer to your target.

▶ Judy wants to swim

Judy liked swimming, but over the past six months she had become down-hearted and unhappy and had not been swimming at all. She listed all of the activities that she wanted to start again, and chose swimming with her friend Susan as her number-one choice. Although she wanted to do it, the thought of going swimming with Susan seemed an enormous challenge. Judy decided to break this task down into the following smaller steps which she felt she could handle.

▶ Step 1. Go to the swimming baths and find out about opening times and cost.

▶ Step 2. Go on her own late one evening for a short 10-minute swim.

▶ Step 3. Go on her own late one evening for a 30-minute swim.

▶ Step 4. Go swimming on her own one morning (when it was busier) for 30 minutes.

▶ Step 5. Go swimming with Susan one morning for 30 minutes.

Breaking the task down into smaller steps made it easier for Judy to be successful.

Face your fears

Breaking tasks down into smaller steps is helpful, but you may still put off doing them because you **feel too anxious**. Anxious feelings often stop us doing the things we would really like to do. However, by not doing them we then have to cope with other unpleasant feelings such as sadness and anger.

▶ You might feel very frightened about going to school, but staying at home might make you feel sad.

▶ You might feel scared about going out with your friends, but staying in on your own might make you feel angry.

At these times it can be useful to *face your fears* and learn to overcome them. You can do this by going through the following steps.

▶ Stage 1. Use **small steps** to break down your challenge into smaller tasks.

▶ Stage 2. Think about **coping self-talk** and practise using it.

▶ Stage 3. **Relax and imagine** yourself successfully coping with your first task.

▶ Stage 4. **Test it out**, one task at a time.

▶ Stage 5. **Praise yourself** for being successful.

▶ Kim is afraid to go out

Kim felt afraid to go out of the house on her own ever since she was pushed over by a gang of boys. She was feeling very unhappy about being trapped in her house but was very scared about going out. She decided to **face her fears**.

▶ *Stage 1.* Kim decided that she would like to be able to go to the shop at the bottom of her road. By using **small steps** she identified the following tasks:

1 to stand by her front gate for a couple of minutes
2 to go outside the gate and then return home
3 to go outside the gate, walk to the bus stop and then return home
4 to walk to the shops (not to go into them) and then return home
5 to walk to the shops and go into them.

▶ *Stage 2.* Kim thought about her **coping self-talk** and as she imagined herself walking to the gate she would say 'I'm safe, no one will hurt me in my garden, I'm going to walk to the gate'.

▶ *Stage 3.* Kim imagined her relaxing place. Once she was **relaxed, she imagined** a picture of herself coming out of the house and calmly walking to the front gate and then returning into her house.

▶ *Stage 4.* After imagining this a few times and practising her coping self-talk, Kim felt ready to **test it out**. She decided that the best time to face her fears was during school-time when she would be less likely to meet any groups of children. She chose the time, relaxed herself, used her coping self-talk and tested her first step.

▶ *Stage 5.* When she came in after being successful, Kim **praised and rewarded** herself with a mug of hot chocolate and a biscuit! She practised this step a few times before moving on to the next one.

Dump your habits

Sometimes our behaviour becomes a problem because there are things we can't stop doing. You may find that you are always:

▶ **checking** – that doors are shut or that lights or taps are turned off

▶ **cleaning** – perhaps your room, or changing your clothes or washing your hands

▶ **counting** – having to repeat things three or four times or doing things in a certain order.

Habits like these are often a way of switching off anxious or unpleasant feelings. The Feeling Finder has helped us to learn that these feelings are usually brought about by our thoughts. For example, we may **think** that if we:

▶ don't constantly check then something bad will happen

▶ don't constantly clean then we might catch germs and diseases or pass these on to others

▶ don't count and do things in a certain order then someone may be hurt.

The habits may make you feel better, but the relief that they bring does not last. It will not be long before the thoughts and unpleasant feelings return and the habits have to be repeated again and again and again.

When this happens, you need to **dump your habits** and prove that anxious feelings can be turned off **without** using your habits.

▶ Step 1. Use **small steps** and put your habits in order, with those that are most difficult to stop at the top, and easier habits at the bottom.

▶ Step 2. **Plan to be successful**.

   1 When will you try your first step?
   2 Plan how you will deal with your unpleasant feelings.
   3 What coping self-talk will you use?
   4 Do you need someone to help you to dump your habits?

▶ Step 3. Try it, but this time **dump your habits** and see how long you can manage without using them. When you start to hold on in this way, use the **Feeling Thermometer** on page 134 to rate how you feel. Keep holding on, **dump your habits**, and keep rating your feelings. You will find that your worrying feelings will start to decrease!

▶ Step 4. Remember to **praise yourself** for being successful.

You will probably need to practise each step a few times. It may also be useful to involve someone else who can help to make sure that you don't use your habits. Once you have been successful, move on to the next step and remember that feelings can be turned off without using habits.

▶ David is worried about germs

David stood in some dog mess and became very worried about germs. He was always cleaning his shoes, and after he had finished doing this he would wash his hands over and over again. If he felt that his hands were dirty, then he would have to clean anything he touched, including his clothes – which he changed three or four times each day. David had finally reached the stage where he wanted to **dump his habits**.

▶ *Step 1*. David used **small steps** and put his habits in order. He thought that the following would be the easiest to stop:

  1 delay changing his clothes for 30 minutes
  2 only change his clothes once a day
  3 limit his hand-washing, and each time wash his hands no more than twice.

The list went on until David reached the final stage of walking around the house in his shoes.

▶ *Step 2*. David **planned to be successful**. He decided that he would keep his mind occupied by using distraction tasks (puzzles), and he practised his coping self-talk: 'I am in charge. I don't need to use these habits to feel good'.

▶ *Step 3*. David tried it. As soon as he felt the need to change his clothes he tried to wait and **dump his habits**. He used the **Feeling Thermometer** and gave himself a fear rating of 8. After 5 minutes his feelings had got worse and had gone up to number 9. He held on, used his **coping self-talk** and tried to relax. After 15 minutes the feelings didn't seem so strong, and his fear rating was now down to 5. He held out for 30 minutes and then changed his clothes.

▶ *Step 4*. David was really **pleased with himself**, and treated himself to a special video.

The next time he tried this he held out for over an hour. The feelings seemed to become less strong even though he didn't use his habits.

► Activity can help you to feel better and gives you less time to listen to your negative thoughts.

► If there are times of the day or week that are difficult, plan your timetable differently.

► Break your challenges down into smaller steps. This will help you to be successful.

► Face your fears and learn to overcome your difficulties.

► If you have problems with checking, cleaning or counting, then learn to dump your habits.

► Keep practising, and reward yourself when you have done well.

CHANGING YOUR BEHAVIOUR

Activity diary

Keep a diary each day of what you have done and how you have felt. Use the Feeling Thermometer on page 134 to rate the strength of these feelings.

Is there any pattern linking what you do and how you feel?

Activity	Feelings
7.00 Morning	
8.00	
9.00	
10.00	
11.00	
12.00	
1.00 Afternoon	
2.00	
3.00	
4.00	
5.00	
6.00	
7.00	
8.00	
9.00	
10.00	
11.00	
12.00	

Next step up the ladder

There are probably lots of things you would like to do. Some of them will seem fairly easy and others will feel more difficult.

Write or draw all of the things you would like to do on a piece of paper. Cut them out and arrange them on the ladder below.

Put those that feel easiest at the bottom, the most difficult ones at the top, and the slightly easier ones in the middle.

Start at the bottom and see if you can complete your next task up the ladder. When you are successful, climb up to the next step and try that one. Taking small steps will help you to climb your ladder.

Hardest

Easiest

Things that make me feel good

Write down or draw the places, activities or people that make you feel good.

Things that make me feel unpleasant

Write down or draw the places, activities or people that make you feel unpleasant.

CHANGING YOUR BEHAVIOUR

Things I would like to do

Write down or draw the things that you would like to do and the things you would like to do more often.

Face your fears

My challenge is:

Stage 1. Use **small steps** to break down your challenge into easier stages.

My steps to success are:

Stage 2. What is your **coping self-talk?**

Stage 3. **Relax and imagine** yourself being successful. Repeat your coping self-talk as you imagine successfully achieving your first step. Practise this a few times.

Stage 4. Choose a time when you will face your fear, relax and **test it out**. Remember to use your coping self-talk.

Stage 5. **Praise and reward** yourself for being successful.

You may want to practise each step a few times, but once you feel confident move on to the next one, and repeat each step until you have overcome your fear.

Small steps

Sometimes tasks or challenges seem too big. When this happens, we need to break them down into smaller steps. This will make each step more possible and help you to be successful.

> **What is your task or challenge?**

> **Break your task or challenge down into smaller steps and write them down or draw them in this box.**

> **Look at all of the steps and arrange them in order of difficulty. Put the easiest ones at the bottom of the page and the hardest at the top.**

Start with the easiest step. Once you have been successful, move on to the next. Breaking tasks or challenges down into smaller steps can help you to be successful.

Dump your habits

Stage 1. Use **small steps**. Write down all of your habits and put them in order, with those that are easiest to stop at the bottom, and those that are hardest to stop at the top.

My steps to success are:

Stage 2. **Plan to be successful**.

What is the easiest habit to stop?

When will you try your challenge and dump this habit?

How will you keep calm?

What is your coping self-talk?

Do you need anyone to help you to dump your habits? Who can help?

Stage 3. **Try it and dump your habit.** Use the **Feeling Thermometer** on page 134 to keep rating how you are feeling.

Stage 4. **Praise and reward yourself** for being successful.

Learning to solve problems

Each day brings a new set of problems and challenges. For example:

▶ dealing with being unfairly told off by a teacher

▶ trying to stay in your seat at school

▶ coping with teasing by an annoying brother or sister

▶ negotiating with your parents about staying out late.

When we encounter a problem we have to think about the different ways in which we could deal with it and then make a decision about what we will do or say. Sometimes we make the right choice, while at other times we seem to get it wrong. There will always be times when this happens, but some people seem to make more wrong choices or find it harder to solve problems than others. When this happens it is useful to think about how you are dealing with your problems and whether you could try to solve them in different ways.

Why do problems happen?

There are many reasons why we are unable to solve our problems successfully. Three of these reasons are particularly common.

▶ Acting without thinking

Decisions and choices are sometimes made too quickly. You may rush into something without really thinking through what will happen.

▶ Nick heard his dad say that he had left the shopping in the car. Wanting to be helpful, Nick rushed out and carried all the bags from the back seat of the car into the house. He didn't check with his parents, but if he had he would have found out that their shopping was in the car boot. The bags he brought in were for a party his dad was organizing at work.

▶ Sabrina heard her teacher's instructions to copy her work into her book, and she immediately picked up her pen and started. Unfortunately, she didn't hear the next instruction, which told her to use a pencil and to start her work on a new page.

Nick and Sabrina were both trying to be helpful, but in their rush they created more problems for themselves.

▶ Feelings take over

Strong feelings like anger or anxiety sometimes take over and prevent us from thinking problems through and making the right choices about what we do or say.

▶ Mike became very angry when he was tackled during a game of football, and he kicked the other player. The referee sent Mike off the pitch.

▶ Jenny didn't understand her schoolwork, but was really worried about asking her teacher for help. She didn't ask, she got her homework wrong and she had to stay behind after school and do it again.

Mike knew that if he kicked someone he would be sent off. Jenny knew that if she got her schoolwork wrong she would have to do it again. At the time, Mike and Jenny were not able to think about the consequences of their behaviour. Strong feelings took over and prevented them from thinking these situations through.

▶ Can't see any other solution

The third main reason why we can't solve problems is because we just can't think of another way of doing things. We become very fixed in our ideas and can't see any other solutions.

Learn to stop and think

It is useful to learn a way of dealing with problems which ensures that you don't rush in with the first thing that comes into your head. A helpful approach is the **Stop, Plan and Go** traffic-light system.

> *RED*. Before you do anything, think of the red traffic light and **Stop**.

> *AMBER*. **Plan** and think about what you want to do or say.

> *GREEN*. **Go** with your plan.

The first step is often the hardest, and sometimes you may find it hard to **STOP** yourself from rushing in. Practise imagining a picture of some traffic lights and as you see the red light think to yourself **STOP**. As the light comes on, take a few deep breaths. This may help you to calm down and slow down enough to let you plan and think about what you want to do. The more you practise, the easier it will become.

You can also use this system at school. You can remind yourself by putting red, amber and green coloured strips around a pencil or ruler or on your pencil case. Seeing the strips will help you to think **'Stop, Plan and Go'**, but no one else will know what the strips mean.

Identify different solutions

Sometimes we meet the same problem or challenge every day but often end up making the wrong decision over and over again. When this happens, it is useful to stop and think about all of the different ways in which you can deal with this problem.

Try using the **'OR'** method to find as many possible solutions as you can. Another way of doing this is to take a sheet of paper and write down all of the possible solutions you can think of in two minutes. The idea is to get as many ideas as you can, so don't worry if some of them seem unrealistic or silly.

▶ Billy is ignored

Billy felt that his friends often ignored him, so he used the **'OR'** method to find ways in which he could get his friends to listen to him.

▶ I could talk louder **OR**

▶ shout **OR**

▶ stand in front of their faces so that they would have to listen to me **OR**

▶ keep repeating myself **OR**

▶ talk with one person rather than all the group **OR**

▶ find things to talk about that really interested them **OR**

▶ find a new group of friends!

For Billy, the idea of shouting all the time seemed silly, and changing his group of friends was not really possible. Some of the other ideas he came up with were more useful. Billy decided that he needed to listen more carefully to the things that really interested his friends. He also decided that he would try to talk more with people on their own, rather than trying to join in with the group discussions.

If you find it hard to think of any different ways of dealing with your problems, then it may be useful to talk this over with someone else. Ask how they would deal with your problem, and see if they can suggest some different ideas.

Think through the consequences

Once you have made a list of possible solutions, the next step is to work out which is the best one. Think about the positive and negative consequences of each idea and then choose the one that you think, on balance, will work best. This involves five steps.

1 What is my problem?
2 How could I deal with this problem?
3 What are the positive consequences of each solution?
4 What are the negative consequences of each solution?
5 On balance, what is the best solution?

▶ Marla gets teased

Three girls at school have started to tease Marla and call her names at break-time. On the first day, Marla became very angry and chased after the girls. On the second day, she hit one of the girls and ended up in trouble in front of the head-teacher. On the third day, she called the girls names back, but this seemed to make the name-calling worse. Marla decided to sit down and work out how she would cope with this problem.

My problem: being teased by Emma, Kate and Jo		
What I could do	Positive consequences	Negative consequences
Hit them whenever they call me names OR	Would make me feel better!	I'd get into more trouble I might be suspended from school They might start to hit me
Find a teacher to tell OR	The teacher would sort it out and I wouldn't get into any more trouble	They might tease me even more for telling the teacher I might not be able to find a teacher
Ignore them OR	If I don't react they might get bored	BUT I CAN'T DO IT because they annoy me so much!
Stay away from them at break-times	They can't tease me I won't get into trouble They might find something else to do	This might not always be easy They might come and look for me
On balance, the best way to solve this problem is to stay out of their way at break-times. If they come and find me, I'll move away and move closer to a teacher.		

Thinking this problem through was helpful for Marla. Although hitting the girls made her feel better, she also realized that this had other consequences which were not good. Marla weighed up all of the ideas, and on balance she chose to stay away from the girls at break-times.

Remind yourself what to do

There will be times when, although you know the best way of dealing with your problems, you slip back into your old ways as your new plans are **forgotten**.

If this happens, you need to work out how you can remind yourself to use your new plan. The people in these examples found some very simple ways to help them to remember how to solve their problems.

▶ Michael fiddles with his pencil case

Michael was in trouble every day at school for fiddling with his pencils and pencil case. He wanted to stop this habit, and he problem-solved with his teacher about what he could do. He decided that he might be able to stop fiddling by sitting on his hands when the teacher was speaking. He agreed with his teacher that she would lightly touch his shoulder if Michael forgot. Michael also decided to put his pencil case in his bag, rather than leaving it out on his desk. He stuck a sign on the inside of his pencil case saying 'put me in your bag', to help him to remember.

▶ Jemma's room is always untidy

Jemma was always in trouble at home for having an untidy bedroom. This had become more of a problem for her recently since her parents had stopped her pocket money. Even when she tried to tidy her room, she never seemed to get it right. There was always something she forgot to do. She decided that she had to stop this happening, and she drew up a 'tidy bedroom checklist' which she put on her bedroom wall. She listed all of the things she needed to do to tidy her room.

- ▶ Pick clothes up off the floor.
- ▶ Put dirty clothes in the washing bin.
- ▶ Put clean clothes in drawers and wardrobe.
- ▶ Make bed.
- ▶ Put magazines and books in a tidy pile.
- ▶ Put CDs in their cases.

Jemma agreed a time with her parents when she would tidy her room, and she used the list to make sure that she did not forget to do anything.

▶ Henry gets wound up

Henry had a very quick temper and became very angry – shouting, swearing and sometimes hitting out. He was always fighting, and had recently been suspended from school for two days. Henry problem-solved this with his best friend and decided that he needed to 'bail out' of arguments. He needed to stop and walk away rather than stay and argue. This was not easy for Henry, so his friend agreed that he would help. When Henry started to become angry, his friend would tell him to 'bail out'. This was the signal for Henry to stop, walk away and calm down. Henry's friend was very helpful and, although it was not easy, Henry started to learn that he could deal with arguments in a better way.

Practise getting it right

Learning to deal with problems in new or different ways is not always easy. It can take time, and you may need to practise before you get it right. As with most things, the more you practise the easier it will become.

▶ Imagine yourself changing the ending

Think about your problem and imagine yourself solving it differently. Instead of using your old solutions, **change the ending** and imagine yourself being successful. Choose a quiet time and get a really good picture of your problem situation in your mind.

▶ Describe the scene as well as you can.

▶ Imagine who will be there.

▶ Think about what is going on and what is being said.

▶ Imagine yourself using your new solution and being successful.

▶ Remember to praise yourself for solving your problem so well.

▶ Millie rushes around

Millie was always in trouble at school for rushing around. Sometimes she would knock and push people in her hurry to be first. She decided that she needed to calm down, and that she would count to five before she did anything. Millie imagined herself using this idea at the end of lessons, going into the dining hall and coming in after lunchtime. Imagining herself counting and becoming calm helped her to prepare to use this idea when she got to school.

▶ Practise acting it out

It is useful to practise using your new skills by acting out your problem situations with friends. Try to make the situation as real as possible, and think about who will be there, what will be said and how they will react. Try out different solutions and see what works well.

Acting out problem situations can be good fun, and if you take it in turns you may find that you can learn some useful tips from your friends!

Plan to be successful

Problem-solving is often used to **stop things happening**.

▶ Marla wanted to stop being teased.

▶ Michael wanted his teacher to stop telling him off.

▶ Henry wanted to stop fighting.

Another way to solve problems is to think about the things you want to happen and then **plan how you can be successful**.

▶ Kia wants to sleep over

Kia wanted to sleep at her friend's house but she didn't think her mum would let her. They were having a lot of arguments, and Kia knew that unless this situation changed her mum would not allow a sleepover. Kia problem-solved how this could change. She knew that this would take time, and she saw the main job as stopping the arguments with her mum. Most of these were about Kia not helping around the house, so she decided that she would start to keep her room tidy. She also decided that she would help to lay the table for meals and help with the washing up afterwards. Kia's mother was very surprised and also very pleased. They argued less, and after a week Kia asked her mother if she could sleep over at her friend's house. Her mother agreed, saying that if Kia was now prepared to help around the home, then she should be allowed some special privileges.

Talk yourself through it

Another useful way of learning to solve problems is to ask someone who is successful to talk you through what they do.

▶ Ask them to tell you what they do.

▶ Watch them doing it.

▶ Then talk yourself through your problem.

This can be very helpful for those problems that seem to occur fairly often.

▶ Mike doesn't know what to say to his friends

Mike felt very worried when he met his friends because he often did not know what to talk about. His friend Reuben was very popular and always seemed to know what to say, so Mike asked for his help. Reuben said that when he arrived at school each morning he would go up to his group of friends, say hello and talk about something that had been on television last night, such as a sports match or the latest episode of their favourite TV soap. Reuben went to school with Mike the next day and as they arrived Reuben talked aloud about what he was going to do as Mike watched. The next day, when Mike arrived at school he talked aloud about what he was going to do. 'I'm going to walk across the playground, go up to Max and Errol, say hello and ask if they saw what happened on our favourite TV soap last night'. Mike did this and was pleased to find that he was soon chatting with his friends. The next day he talked himself through it again, and after a few times Mike found that he was now doing this without thinking.

▶ Don't rush – learn to **STOP, PLAN and GO**.

▶ Think about the **different ways** in which you could solve your problem.

▶ Think through the **consequences** of each solution.

▶ On **balance**, choose the best solution.

▶ Ask someone successful to tell you what they do, then watch them and finally **talk yourself through it**.

▶ Find ways to **remind** yourself to use your plans.

Identifying possible solutions

What is my problem?

Write down **ALL** of the possible ways in which you can solve this problem. The idea is to try to find as many different solutions as possible.

1   I could solve this problem by:

2   **OR**

3   **OR**

4   **OR**

5   **OR**

6   **OR**

7   **OR**

Identifying possible solutions

It is useful to find out how other people might solve this problem. Think of someone who you think could help, and ask them what ideas they might suggest.

I asked:

They suggested that I could solve this problem by:

What are the consequences of my solutions?

Write down your problem and list the different solutions you have identified. Think about the negative and positive consequences of each solution and write these down. When you have finished, look at your list and on balance choose the best solution for your problem.

My problem is:

Possible solution	Positive consequences	Negative consequences
1		
2		
3		
4		
5		
6		
7		

On balance, the best way of solving this problem is:

Looking for solutions

Write down or draw your problem and fill in all of the possible solutions you can think of.

Talk yourself through it

If you find that the same problem occurs over and over again, then find out how someone else copes, watch them do it and then talk yourself through their plan for success.

What is my problem?

Who could I talk with who is successful?

How do they deal with this problem?

When can I watch them talk me through their plan?

Talk yourself through it

When shall I try to use this plan?

What will I say to myself?

How am I going to reward myself for being successful?

How did it go?

Stop, plan and go

Use the traffic lights to help you to plan how you will deal with your problem.

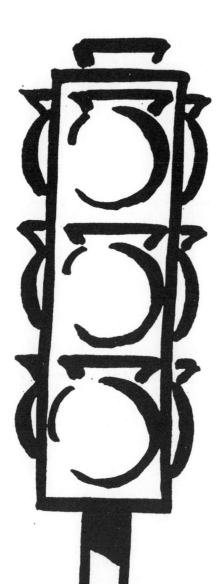

STOP. What is your problem?

PLAN. What is your solution?

GO. When will you try it out?

References

Bandura, A. (1977) *Social learning theory*. Prentice-Hall, Englewood Cliffs, NJ.

Barrett, P.M. (1998) Evaluation of cognitive-behavioural group treatments for childhood anxiety disorders. *Journal of Clinical Child Psychology* **27**, 459–68.

Barrett, P.M., Dadds, M.R. and Rapee, R.M. (1996) Family treatment of childhood anxiety: a controlled trial. *Journal of Consulting and Clinical Psychology* **64**, 333–42.

Beck, A.T. (1976) *Cognitive therapy and the emotional disorders*. International Universities Press, New York.

Beck, A.T., Emery, G. and Greenberg, R.L. (1985) *Anxiety disorders and phobias: a cognitive perspective*. Basic Books, New York.

Beck, A.T., Rush, A.J., Shaw, B.F. and Emery, G. (1979) *Cognitive therapy for depression*. Guildford Press, New York.

Belsher, G. and Wilkes, T.C.R. (1994) Ten key principles of adolescent cognitive therapy. In: Wilkes, T.C.R., Belsher, G., Rush, A.J. and Frank, E. (eds), *Cognitive therapy for depressed adolescents*. Guildford Press, New York.

Bodiford, C.A., Eisenstadt, R.H., Johnson, J.H. and Bradlyn, A.S. (1988) Comparison of learned helpless cognitions and behaviour in children with high and low scores on the Children's Depression Inventory. *Journal of Clinical Child Psychology* **17**, 152–8.

Burns, D.D. (1980) *Feeling good*. New American Library, New York.

Chandler, M.J. (1973) Egocentrism and antisocial behaviour: the assessment and training of social perspective-taking skills. *Developmental Psychology* **9**, 326–32.

Cobham, V.E., Dadds, M.R. and Spence, S.H. (1998) The role of parental anxiety in the treatment of childhood anxiety. *Journal of Consulting and Clinical Psychology*, **66**, 6, 893–905.

Cohen, J.A. and Mannarino, A.P. (1996) A treatment outcome study for sexually abused preschool children: initial findings. *Journal of the American Academy of Child and Adolescent Psychiatry* **35**, 42–50.

Cohen, J.A. and Mannarino, A.P. (1998) Interventions for sexually abused children: initial treatment outcome findings. *Child Maltreatment* **3**, 17–26.

Curry, J.F. and Craighead, W.E. (1990) Attributional style in clinically depressed and conduct-disordered adolescents. *Journal of Clinical and Consulting Psychology* **58**, 109–16.

Dadds, M.R., Spence, S.H., Holland, D.E., Barrett, P.M. and Laurens, K.R. (1997) Prevention and early intervention for anxiety disorders: a controlled trial. *Journal of Consulting and Clinical Psychology* **65**, 627–35.

Deblinger, E., McLeer, S.V. and Henry, D. (1990) Cognitive behavioural treatment for sexually abused children suffering post-traumatic stress disorder: preliminary findings. *Journal of the American Academy of Child and Adolescent Psychiatry* **29**, 747–52.

Dodge, K.A. (1985) Attributional bias in aggressive children. In: Kendall, P.C. (ed.), *Advances in cognitive-behavioural research and therapy. Volume 4*. Academic Press, New York.

Doherr, E.A., Corner, J.M. and Evans, E. (1999) *Pilot study of young children's abilities to use the concepts central to cognitive behavioural therapy*. Unpublished manuscript. University of East Anglia, Norwich.

Douglas, J. (1998) Therapy for parents of difficult pre-school children. In: Graham, P. (ed.), *Cognitive behaviour therapy for children and families*. Cambridge University Press, Cambridge.

Durlak, J.A., Furnham, T. and Lampman, C. (1991) Effectiveness of cognitive-behaviour therapy for maladapting children: a meta-analysis. *Psychological Bulletin* **110**, 204–14.

Durlak, J.A., Wells, A.M., Cotton, J.K. and Johnson, S. (1995) Analysis of selected methodological issues in child psychotherapy research. *Journal of Clinical Child Psychology* **24**, 141–8.

Ehlers, A. and Clark, D.M. (2000) A cognitive model of post-traumatic stress disorder. *Behaviour Research and Therapy* **38**, 319–45.

Ellis, A. (1962) *Reason and emotion in psychotherapy*. Lyle-Stewart, New York.

Fennel, M. (1989) Depression. In: Hawton, K., Salkovskis, P.M., Kirk, J. and Clark, D.M. (eds), *Cognitive behaviour therapy for psychiatric problems. A practical guide*. Oxford Medical Publications, Oxford.

Fielstein, E., Klein, M.S., Fischer, M., Hanon, C., Koburger, P., Schneider, M.J. and Leitenberg, H. (1985) Self-esteem and causal attributions for success and failure in children. *Cognitive Therapy and Research* **9**, 381–98.

Graham, P. (1998) *Cognitive behaviour therapy for children and families*. Cambridge University Press, Cambridge.

Greenberg, D. and Padesky, C. (1995) *Mind over mood*. Guildford Press, New York.

Harrington, R., Wood, A. and Verduyn, C. (1998) Clinically depressed adolescents. In: Graham, P. (ed.), *Cognitive behaviour therapy for children and families*. Cambridge University Press, Cambridge.

Harrington, R., Whittaker, J., Shoebridge, P. and Campbell, F. (1998) Systematic review of efficacy of cognitive behaviour therapies in childhood and adolescent depressive disorder. *British Medical Journal* **316**, 1559–63.

Hawton, K., Salkovskis, P.M., Kirk, J. and Clark, D.M. (1989) *Cognitive behaviour therapy for psychiatric problems: a practical guide*. Oxford Medical Publications, Oxford.

Herbert, M. (1998) Adolescent conduct disorders. In: Graham, P. (ed.), *Cognitive behaviour therapy for children and families*. Cambridge University Press, Cambridge.

Hobday, A. and Ollier, K. (1998) *Creative therapy: activities with children and adolescents*. British Psychological Society, Leicester.

Hughes, J.N. (1988) *Cognitive behaviour therapy with children in schools*. Pergamon Press, New York.

Jackson, H.J. and King, N.J. (1981) The emotive imagery treatment of a child's trauma-induced phobia. *Journal of Behaviour Therapy and Experimental Psychiatry* **12**, 325–8.

Kane, M.T. and Kendall, P.C. (1989) Anxiety disorders in children: a multiple baseline evaluation of a cognitive behavioural treatment. *Behaviour Therapy* **20**, 499–508.

Kaplan, C.A., Thompson, A.E. and Searson, S.M. (1995) Cognitive behaviour therapy in children and adolescents. *Archives of Disease in Childhood* **73**, 472–5.

Kazdin, A.E. and Weisz, J.R. (1998) Identifying and developing empirically supported child and adolescent treatments. *Journal of Consulting and Clinical Psychology* **66**, 19–36.

Kendall, P.C. (1991) Guiding theory for treating children and adolescents. In: Kendall, P.C. (ed.), *Child and adolescent therapy: cognitive-behavioural procedures*. Guildford Press, New York.

Kendall, P.C., Kane, M., Howard, B. and Siqueland, L. (1992) *Cognitive-behaviour therapy for anxious children: treatment manual*. Workbook Publishing, Ardmore, PA.

Kendall, P.C. (1993) Cognitive-behavioural therapies with youth: guiding theory, current status and emerging developments. *Journal of Consulting and Clinical Psychology* **61**, 235–47.

Kendall, P.C. (1994) Treating anxiety disorders in children: results of a randomised clinical trial. *Journal of Consulting and Clinical Psychology* **62**, 100–10.

Kendall, P.C. and Chansky, T.E. (1991) Considering cognition in anxiety-disordered youth. *Journal of Anxiety Disorders* **5**, 167–85.

Kendall, P.C. and Hollon, S.D. (eds) (1979) *Cognitive-behavioural interventions: theory, research and procedures*. Academic Press, New York.

Kendall, P.C. and Panichelli-Mindel, S.M. (1995) Cognitive-behavioural treatments. *Journal of Abnormal Child Psychology* **23**, 107–24.

Kendall, P.C., Stark, K.D. and Adam, T. (1990) Cognitive deficit or cognitive distortion in childhood depression. *Journal of Abnormal Child Psychology* **18**, 255–70.

Kendall, P.C., Flannery-Schroeder, E., Panichelli-Mindel, S.M., Sotham-Gerow, M., Henin, A. and Warman, M. (1997) Therapy with youths with anxiety disorders: a second randomized clinical trial. *Journal of Consulting and Clinical Psychology* **65**, 366–80.

Kendall, P.C., Chansky, T.E., Friedaman, M., Kim, R.S., Kortlander, E., Conan, K.R., Sessa, F.M. and Siqueland, L. (1992) *Anxiety disorders in youth: cognitive behavioural interventions*. Allyn and Bacon, Needham Heights, MA.

King, N.J., Molloy, G.N., Heyme, D., Murphy, G.C. and Ollendick, T. (1998) Emotive imagery treatment for childhood phobias: a credible and empirically validated intervention? *Behavioural and Cognitive Psychotherapy* **26**, 103–13.

King, N.J., Tonge, B.J., Heyne, D., Pritchard, M., Rollings, S., Young, D., Myerson, N. and Ollendick, T.H. (1998) Cognitive behavioural treatment of school-refusing children: a controlled evaluation. *Journal of the American Academy of Child and Adolescent Psychiatry* **37**, 395–403.

Lazarus, A.A. and Abramovitz, A. (1962) The use of 'emotive imagery' in the treatment of children's phobias. *Journal of Mental Science* **108**, 191–5.

Leitenberg, H., Yost, L.W. and Carroll-Wilson, M. (1986) Negative cognitive errors in children: questionnaire development, normative data, and comparisons between children with and without self-reported symptoms of depression, low self-esteem and evaluation anxiety. *Journal of Consulting and Clinical Psychology* **54**, 528–36.

Lewinsohn, P.M. and Clarke, G.N. (1999) Psychosocial treatments for adolescent depression. *Clinical Psychology Review* **19**, 329–42.

Lochman, J.E., White, K.J. and Wayland, K.K. (1991) Cognitive-behavioural assessment and treatment with aggressive children. In: Kendall, P.C. (ed.), *Child and adolescent therapy: cognitive-behavioural procedures*. Guildford Press, New York.

March, J.S. (1995) Cognitive-behavioral psychotherapy for children and adolescents with OCD: a review and recommendations for treatment. *Journal of the American Academy of Child and Adolescent Psychiatry* **34**, 7–17.

March, J.S., Mulle, K. and Herbel, B. (1994) Behavioural psychotherapy for children and adolescents with obsessive-compulsive disorder: an open clinical trial of a new protocol-driven treatment package. *Journal of the American Academy of Child and Adolescent Psychiatry* **33**, 333–41.

March, J.S., Amaya-Jackson, L., Murray, M.C. and Schulte, A. (1998) Cognitive behavioural psychotherapy for children and adolescents with post-traumatic stress disorder after a single incident stressor. *Journal of the American Academy of Child and Adolescent Psychiatry* **37**, 585–93.

Meichenbaum, D.H. (1975) Self-instructional methods. In: Kanfer, F.H. and Goldstein, A.P. (eds), *Helping people change: a textbook of methods*. Pergamon, New York.

Miller, W.R. and Rollnick, S. (1991) *Motivational interviewing*. Plenum Press, New York.

Perry, D.G., Perry, L.C. and Rasmussen, P. (1986) Cognitive social learning mediators of aggression. *Child Development* **57**, 700–11.

Rehm, L.P. and Carter, A.S. (1990) Cognitive components of depression. In: Lewis, M. and Miller, S.M. (eds), *Handbook of developmental psychopathology*. Plenum Press, New York.

Ronen, T. (1992) Cognitive therapy with young children. *Child Psychotherapy and Human Development* **23**, 19–30.

Ronen, T. (1993) Intervention package for treating encopresis in a 6-year-old boy: a case study. *Behavioural Psychotherapy* **21**, 127–35.

Ronen, T., Rahav, G. and Wozner, Y. (1995) Self-control and enuresis. *Journal of Cognitive Psychotherapy: an International Quarterly* **9**, 249–58.

Rosenstiel, A.K. and Scott, D.S. (1977) Four considerations in using imagery techniques with children. *Journal of Behaviour Therapy and Experimental Psychiatry* **8**, 287–90.

Roth, A. and Fonagy, P. (1996) *What works for whom: a critical review of psychotherapy research*. Guildford Press, New York.

Royal College of Psychiatry (1997) *Behavioural and cognitive treatments: guidance for good practice*. Council Report CR68. Royal College of Psychiatry, London.

Salkovskis, P. (1999) Understanding and treating obsessive-compulsive disorder. *Behaviour Research and Therapy* **37**, 29–52.

Salmon, K. and Bryant, R. (2002) Posttraumatic stress disorder in children: The influence of developmental factors. *Clinical Psychology Review*, **22**, 163–188.

Sanders, M.R., Shepherd, R.W., Cleghorn, G. and Woolford, H. (1994) The treatment of recurrent abdominal pain in children: a controlled comparison of cognitive-behavioural family intervention and standard pediatric care. *Journal of Consulting and Clinical Psychology* **62**, 306–14.

Schmidt, N.B., Joiner, T.E., Young, J.E. and Telch, M.J. (1995) The schema questionnaire: investigation of psychometric properties and the hierarchical structure of a measure of maladaptive schemas. *Cognitive Therapy and Research* **19**, 295–321.

Schmidt, U. (1998) Eating disorders and obesity. In: Graham, P. (ed.), *Cognitive behaviour therapy for children and families*. Cambridge University Press, Cambridge.

Skinner, B.F. (1974) *About behaviorism*. Cape, London.

Silverman, W.K., Kurtines, W.M., Ginsburg, G.S., Weems, C.F., Lumpkin, P.W. and Carmichael, D.H. (1999a) Treating anxiety disorders in children with group cognitive behavioural therapy: a randomized clinical trial. *Journal of Consulting and Clinical Psychology* **67**, 995–1003.

Silverman, W.K., Kurtines, W.M., Ginsburg, G.S., Weems, C.F., Rabian, B. and Setafini, L.T. (1999b) Contingency management, self-control and education support in the treatment of childhood phobic disorders: a randomized clinical trial. *Journal of Consulting and Clinical Psychology* **67**, 675–87.

Smith, P., Perrin, S. and Yule, W. (1999) Cognitive behaviour therapy for post-traumatic stress disorder. *Child Psychology and Psychiatry Review* **4**, 177–82.

Spence, S.H. (1994) Practitioner review. Cognitive therapy with children and adolescents: from theory to practice. *Journal of Child Psychology and Psychiatry* **37**, 1191–228.

Spence, S. and Donovan, C. (1998) Interpersonal problems. In: Graham, P. (ed.), *Cognitive behaviour therapy for children and families.* Cambridge University Press, Cambridge.

Spence, S., Donovan, C. and Brechman-Toussaint, M. (1999) Social skills, social outcomes and cognitive features of childhood social phobia. *Journal of Abnormal Psychology* **108**, 211–21.

Spence, S., Donovan, C. and Brechman-Toussaint, M. (2000) The treatment of childhood social phobia: the effectiveness of a social skills training-based cognitive behavioural intervention with and without parental involvement. *Journal of Child Psychology and Psychiatry* **41**, 713–26.

Spivack, G. and Shure, M.B. (1974) *Social adjustment of young children. A cognitive approach to solving real-life problems.* Jossey Bass, London.

Spivack, G., Platt, J.J. and Shure, M.B. (1976) *The problem-solving approach to adjustment.* Jossey Bass, San Francisco, CA.

Sunderland, M. and Engleheart, P. (1993) *Draw on your emotions.* Inslow Press Ltd, Bicester.

Turk, J. (1998) Children with learning difficulties and their parents. In: Graham, P. (ed.), *Cognitive behaviour therapy for children and families.* Cambridge University Press, Cambridge.

Toren, P., Wolmer, L., Rosental, B., Eldar, S., Koren, S., Lask, M., Weizman, R. and Laor, N. (2000) Case series: brief parent–child group therapy for childhood anxiety disorders using a manual-based cognitive-behavioural technique. *Journal of the American Academy of Child and Adolescent Psychiatry* **39**, 1309–12.

Verduyn, C. (2000) Cognitive behaviour therapy in childhood depression. *Child Psychology and Psychiatry Review* **5**, 176–80.

Wallace, S.A., Crown, J.M., Cox, A.D. and Berger, M. (1995) *Epidemiologically based needs assessment: child and adolescent mental health.* Wessex Institute of Public Health, Winchester.

Weisz, J.R., Donenburg, G.R., Han, S.S. and Weiss, B. (1995) Bridging the gap between laboratory and clinic in child and adolescent psychotherapy. *Journal of Consulting and Clinical Psychology* **63**, 688–701.

Whitaker, S. (2001) Anger control for people with learning disabilities: a critical review. *Behavioural and Cognitive Psychotherapy* **29**, 277–93.

Wolpe, J. (1958) *Psychotherapy by reciprocal inhibition.* Stanford University Press, Stanford, CA.

Young, J. (1990) *Cognitive therapy for personality disorders: a schema-focused approach.* Professional Resource Press, Sarasota, FL.

Young, J. and Brown, P.F. (1996) Cognitive behaviour therapy for anxiety: practical tips for using it with children. *Clinical Psychology Forum* **91**, 19–21.

Index